ELVIS PRESLEY

UNSEEN ARCHIVES

ELVIS PRESLEY

UNSEEN ARCHIVES

Marie Clayton

p

This is a Parragon Book
This edition published in 2006

Parragon
Queen Street House, 4 Queen Street
Bath, BA1 1HE, UK

Text © Parragon Books Ltd 2003
For details of photographs, see pages 382–383

Produced by Atlantic Publishing
Design and origination by Cambridge Publishing Management Ltd
Cover designed by Tony Collins

ISBN Hardback 1 40546 779 7
ISBN Paperback 1 40546 782 7

Printed in Indonesia

CONTENTS

INTRODUCTION

Elvis Presley burst onto the American music scene in 1956, although he had been well-known locally around Memphis for some time beforehand. He quickly became synonymous with the new rock 'n' roll music and teenagers everywhere took him to their hearts. His sensual performing style whipped his female fans into a frenzy, which initially caused much criticism in the press – but the resulting publicity did his career no harm at all. After he was drafted and did his service in the US army, without complaint or favours, opinion about him in the press began to change, and on his return his new, mature style helped him to reach an even wider audience.

Not content with being perhaps the world's most popular singer, he also moved into acting and soon took Hollywood by storm. During his career he made 31 films – all of which were a success at the box office – and in the middle of the 1960s he was the highest-paid actor in Hollywood. After he returned to the concert stage in the 1970s his shows in Las Vegas were legendary, and he was soon dubbed the 'World's Greatest Entertainer'.

Elvis Presley: Unseen Archives charts the fascinating life of Elvis, right from his humble beginnings to his tragic death as a superstar and its aftermath. The exciting collection of photographs featured not only show him performing, but also include candid shots documenting his private life and a comprehensive selection of stills taken during the making of his films. Many of the photographs are not clearly dated in the archives, but in this book they have been carefully placed in context with what was happening in his career at around the time they were taken. The pictures are accompanied by detailed and perceptive captions, which give a rounded portrait of the world's most famous singer. Elvis Presley was a phenomenon and his legacy continues to captivate people even today – the King may be dead, but his memory lingers on.

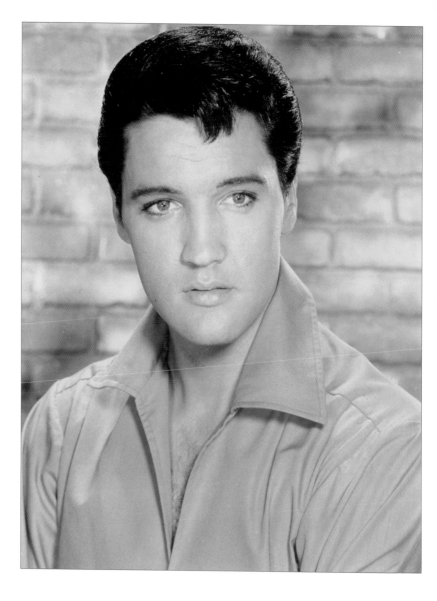

ELVIS PRESLEY

UNSEEN ARCHIVES

CHAPTER ONE

Love Me Tender

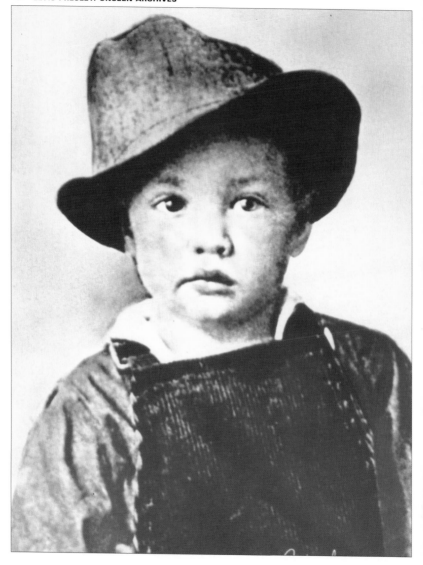

When Elvis Presley was born on 8 January 1935, few people could have predicted that he would go on to live the 'American dream'. His family were so poor they could not afford adequate medical care; as a result his older twin brother, Jesse, was stillborn – a loss that was never to be forgotten, either by his mother, Gladys, or by Elvis himself. In the following years the family moved around Mississippi. Vernon, Elvis's father, had a series of jobs and Gladys often had to work to support the family; and, when things got too tough, they simply moved on. Elvis was very close to his mother – particularly after his father was imprisoned for several months for forging a cheque – and she was very protective of her only surviving child.

Elvis grew up in a series of homes close to black neighbourhoods and, as a result, enjoyed black R&B, jazz and soul music from his earliest years, never regarding it as something separate from his own life as most white people did at the time. His family was closely involved with the church – particularly Gladys, who often attended several times a day – and Elvis was brought up to the sounds of gospel music, joining in as soon as he was able. Gladys also listened to country and western music on the radio at home, and Elvis was quick to learn all the songs.

Despite their circumstances, Gladys insisted that Elvis learn good manners and show respect to his elders – a grounding that stayed with him for the rest of his life. She constantly impressed upon him that he was special and different from other people. He grew up rather shy and dreamy, something of a loner, and music became a release from the constraints of his life. His family had no money to pay for lessons so he taught himself to play the piano and learned guitar from family friends. With a good memory for words and music, he was able to sing or play a song after hearing it just once or twice. He entered his first singing competition at the age of 10, coming second and winning five dollars plus free admission to some fairground rides.

Moving to Memphis in 1948, the Presleys lived near Beale Street, the legendary home of the blues. Moving his body while he was singing was something Elvis had already learned from gospel singers but, in Memphis, he also learned from the way the black singers he saw there moved. He came to admire their sense of style and colour, and in his teens began to develop his own look, which combined bold colours and sharp tailoring with long, slicked-back hair and sideburns. Typical outfits included a bolero jacket bought from Lanskys – a tailor on Beale Street – and trousers with a bright stripe down the side of the leg, and a bright-pink suit teamed with white suede shoes. It was very different from the cropped, preppy look of most other teenagers of the time. At first, Elvis aspired to be a gospel singer, but he also played hillbilly music and soon developed his own sound – a sound that was unlike that of any of the well-known singers of the time, but that later became known as rockabilly and then rock 'n' roll.

Sam Phillips and Marion Keisker had opened a recording studio in Memphis, mainly to record the music played by black artists. Sometime during the summer of 1953, Elvis – by that time working as a truck driver – turned up on their doorstep to record something and to let Sam hear him sing. Nothing happened for some time, but eventually Sam called him back and teamed him up with two more experienced musicians: guitarist Scotty Moore and bass player Bill Black. After a lot of rehearsing and several false starts as they found their way together, the three of them recorded an old blues number by Arthur 'Big Boy' Crudup: 'That's All Right, Mama'. A few days later, Dewey Phillips – one of the most popular and influential disc jockeys in the area – played the record around 14 times in just one evening (the exact number is uncertain) and told his listeners it was sure to be a hit. The results stunned everybody: thousands of phone calls requested more of the new singer and, much to Sam Phillips's surprise, Elvis's music was not only popular with the white audience, but with the black one too.

At first, Scotty Moore managed the group, but later, DJ Bob Neal took over, making bookings for live appearances at clubs and concerts, and later organizing local concert tours. They began to play regularly at the Eagle's Nest in Memphis, but Sam Phillips also managed to get a booking at that mecca of country singing, Nashville's Grand Ole Opry. It was unheard of for an unknown singer to play the Opry, and all of them were thrilled; unfortunately, though, the audience was not ready for their new style and Elvis was advised to stick to driving trucks. He never played there again. The Louisiana Hayride, broadcast on KWKH from Shreveport's Municipal Auditorium, proved more welcoming. Elvis and the Blue Moon Boys were an instant hit and were quickly invited back. They began to tour almost full-time – often driving all night, playing a concert, then driving on to the next show with just a few snatched hours of sleep in the back of the car. Despite this, Elvis seemed constantly active and rarely tired; when he finally did sleep, though, it would be for 11 or 12 hours.

Now that he was releasing records and playing regularly at the Louisiana Hayride and other well-known venues, Elvis began to feel he was really on his way. He already had a large group of fans who would arrive whenever he was due to appear. He was still a local phenomenon, however, and needed another push to achieve national popularity. That push was not long coming. In late 1954, Elvis met Colonel Tom Parker for the first time, who soon had plans for the still rather naive young singer who was driving audiences wild.

The Colonel had started out in carnival, but moved into showbusiness when he became the manager of singer Eddy Arnold. When he met Elvis, he was working as a promoter, and his astute business practices, promotional skills and attention

to detail were already famous. Although his title was an honorary one, conferred by a state governor, he insisted on using it at all times. Having arranged a few tours for Elvis and noting the audience reaction, he began to take over, manoeuvring everyone else out of the way.

With the Colonel's help, Elvis transferred to the national stage and was soon headlining shows across the country. Women went wild as he shook his hips or jiggled his legs – movements a world away from those of other singers of the time, who hardly moved at all while they sang. Some religious leaders took exception to his 'lewd' performance, and called for both Elvis and his music to be banned. At a concert in Jacksonville, Florida, in May 1955, fans rioted, leaping onto the stage and attempting to tear off Elvis's clothes; this soon became a fairly regular occurrence. Elvis loved all the attention and often encouraged his fans – both onstage and off. Despite his polite, shy and humble image, Elvis had a reputation for never turning a woman away from his door. He had been quick to realize that women liked him and that it was easy to persuade them to join him in bed. He dated several different women regularly – even when his steady girlfriend, Dixie Locke, was still waiting for him at home. She eventually split up with him, although not because of the time he spent with his other women; she was dismayed that the demands of touring left him with no time to spend with her.

Gladys had always wanted her son Elvis to be someone special, but now that he was, she found it hard to cope with his fame. He was always away touring instead of at home with her, and she was distressed by the overheated reaction of

Opposite: The second Sun single, 'Good Rockin' Tonight' was as great a success as the first. Elvis, Scotty Moore and Bill Black soon had regular concert bookings and Sam Phillips arranged for them to appear on Nashville's Grand Ole Opry.

his female fans. Elvis had been her main emotional support for many years; now he was no longer around and her problems began to escalate.

By November 1955, Colonel Parker had arranged for RCA to buy Elvis's contract from Sam Phillips, who needed funds to develop his other singers – including Johnny Cash, Roy Orbison, Carl Perkins and Jerry Lee Lewis. The following year RCA released its first Elvis single, 'Heartbreak Hotel'. To the disappointment of RCA executives, it was a very different sound to anything Elvis had recorded before and they began to wonder if they had made a costly mistake. However, it was a massive hit, going to No. 1 in the charts and, by mid-1956, Elvis was bringing in over half of RCA's total income.

Elvis also made several appearances on *Stage Show* on CBS TV, reaching an audience across the entire country for the first time. The Colonel soon became Elvis's sole and exclusive manager. He had recognized that Elvis appealed to a new audience, as the repressed youth of America found their own identity and began to rebel against authority. Naturally, these teenagers wanted their own music, preferably something their elders did not approve of, and rock 'n' roll fitted the bill perfectly. With this audience came a vast new market just waiting to be tapped. Part of Elvis's appeal was that he was a mass of contradictions: he appeared shy and polite but, onstage, moved in a way that drove women crazy; he belted out rock 'n' roll numbers but sang gospel with true feeling; he was quietly spoken and loved his mother, but was also an audacious youth who encouraged teenagers to rebel.

Elvis himself could never understand why there was a problem. He moved the way he did because that was what seemed natural to him; gospel was his own first love, but rock 'n' roll was what the audience wanted; and he never saw himself as a rebel because he had simply grown up with the kind of music he sang. Record sales boomed on the back of all the publicity. The Colonel already had his eye on the next move and, in April 1956, Elvis did a screen test and soon had a movie contract with Paramount Pictures.

Despite everything else that was going on, Elvis was still touring almost non-stop – including a two-week run at the New Frontier Hotel in Las Vegas. Unfortunately, this was not a success as the venue's middle-class audience was more used to sophisticated entertainers like Frank Sinatra and didn't take to the raw energy of Elvis's rock 'n' roll. However, it was in Vegas that Elvis met Liberace, who was to become a close friend, and who advised him on how to dress to please his audience. Elvis's style soon began to change, and he not only solved his skin problems but also had his teeth capped.

In August 1956, Elvis began work on his first film, *Love Me Tender*, a drama set just after the Civil War. Elvis played the youngest son of a farming family, who marries the girlfriend of his eldest brother after everyone assumes that the brother is dead. When the older brother returns, the family is torn apart and Elvis's character is killed. The movie co-stars Debra Paget and Richard Egan; Elvis appears again at the end, singing the title song over the credits. The Colonel was astute enough to retain the publishing rights to the movie's score, rather than handing them over to the studio, and after Elvis appeared on *The Ed Sullivan Show*, advance orders of two million were received for the single 'Love Me Tender'. The picture opened in 500 cinemas that November and was a huge hit, despite an unenthusiastic response from the film critics.

The Colonel was also quick to realize the potential for Elvis-related merchandise, and set up companies to sell a Presley product range that included jeans, charm bracelets, stick-on sideburns, hair oil, bubblegum cards and even lipstick. At the center of all this fuss, however, Elvis was becoming increasingly isolated, his movements restricted. He was already beginning to acquire the habits that would eventually lead to his destruction.

The Hillbilly Cat...

Elvis takes a turn at the drums. At first, he was backed on stage only by Scotty on lead guitar
and Bill on bass, but after they decided to hire a full-time drummer they were joined by DJ
Fontana. As a musician, Elvis was largely self-taught. His parents did not have the money to pay
for lessons, but he grew up surrounded by music and quickly learned to carry a tune.

Accomplished pianist

Although he rarely played in public, Elvis was also an accomplished pianist. He usually played for himself or close friends, and only when he felt happy and at ease. He often played gospel music for pleasure and thought about becoming a gospel singer, but rockabilly – the early form of rock 'n' roll – was what the audience wanted.

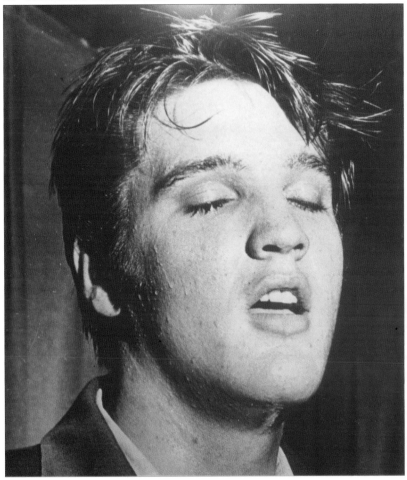

Elvis soon developed a huge following that mainly consisted of teenage girls, and by mid 1955 his devoted army of fans would attend wherever he was performing. Elvis loved the attention and was quick to encourage the girls in the audience, teasing and swivelling his hips until they became so hysterical they would try to grab him before he left the stage. Their jealous boyfriends could be even more dangerous.

Top: An early studio portrait – after Elvis met Liberace in Las Vegas, he made many changes to the way he looked. Liberace had told him that he should dress to please the audience, and Elvis took his advice to heart.

Bottom: Belting out a song on stage. The release of 'Baby, Let's Play House' caused a major stir because of its suggestive lyrics, but the fans loved it and it quickly went into the national charts – the first Elvis record to do so. Soon afterwards, Elvis signed a management contract with Colonel Tom Parker.

Presley

The King of Rock 'n' Roll

After he began to become well known nationally, almost every aspect of Elvis was publicly criticized – his dress, the raunchy way he moved, his ducktail hair, his sideburns. Because of all this negative publicity he soon developed an image as a dangerous rebel, who would encourage young people to defy their elders – but teenagers loved him partly because their elders did disapprove. Elvis himself could never understand the fuss; he did not try to cause offence and almost everyone who met him was soon won over by his quiet, shy charm. The Colonel could see the power of the new teenage market and for a while was content to exploit it – he created all kinds of gimmicks to keep the fans happy and the free publicity also boosted record sales.

After he signed with RCA at the end of 1955, Elvis began to move away from rockabilly into true rock 'n' roll. It was the start of a gradual progression in his style and in his music, always moving on to try and reach a wider audience. How much of this was a natural progression and how much was manipulated by Colonel Parker is open to debate.

Lifelong friends

Elvis first appeared in Las Vegas in April 1956, but the engagement was not a great success. However, he met Liberace there for the first time and the two of them went on to become lifelong friends.

Heartbreak Hotel

Released in 1956, 'Heartbreak Hotel' was the first Elvis record that became a hit for RCA. Elvis had first heard the song in 1955 at a disc jockey convention and had immediately decided he wanted to record it. Songwriters Mae Axton and Tommy Durden had written the song after reading a newspaper article about a young man who had committed suicide, leaving a note that said, 'I walk a lonely street'. The song was very different from the material Elvis had previously recorded, but it went on to become the first of his records to sell a million copies and his first No. 1 hit.

Opposite: Irish McCalla, the star of *Sheena, Queen of the Jungle*, holds Elvis hostage. The two of them appeared together on *The Milton Berle Show* in spring 1956.

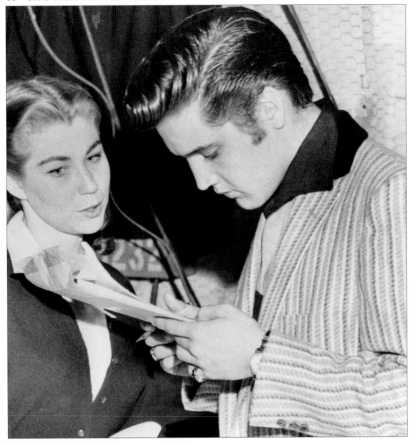

Speculating about romance

Judy Powell Spreckels, former wife of sugar heir Adolph Spreckels, manages to catch Elvis after *The Milton Berle Show*. The two of them exchanged rings, and the press speculated that they were enjoying a romance.

Opposite: *The Milton Berle Show* that featured Elvis's first appearance was broadcast from the deck of the USS *Hancock*, which was docked at the San Diego Naval Station. Despite the novelty of the location, it was his second appearance on the show in June of that year that brought more publicity.

Hound Dog

During his second appearance on *The Milton Berle Show*, Elvis sang 'Hound Dog' for the first time on television. It was a new song, but the audience loved it and Elvis responded to their enthusiasm by taking his hip-swivelling performance to greater heights. 'Hound Dog' was released in July 1956 and sold over five million copies by the end of the year.

Topping the ratings

As he reached the final part of 'Hound Dog', Elvis slowed down the tempo of the song and proceeded to thrust his hips in time to the music in a distinctly suggestive way. The studio audience were driven to a frenzy of excitement, screaming and laughing at the same time. That evening, for the first time in the season, *The Milton Berle Show* topped *Sergeant Bilko* in the ratings.

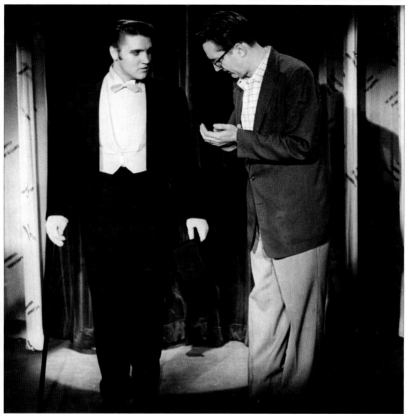

Fans furious at critics' response

Soon afterwards Elvis appeared on the *Steve Allen Show*, but Allen insisted his performance be toned down and that he should wear a tuxedo. The fans were furious, and picketed the NBC studios the following morning.

Opposite: The day after *The Milton Berle Show* was broadcast, many critics condemned Elvis's performance. John Crosby of the *New York Herald Tribune* said he was 'unspeakably untalented and vulgar', Jack O'Brian of the *New York Journal-American* wrote of '…a display of primitive physical movement difficult to describe in terms suitable to a family newspaper…', and Ben Gross said in the *Daily News* that '…he gave an exhibition that was suggestive and vulgar, tinged with the kind of animalism that should be confined to dives and bordellos.'

A new, confident Elvis

On stage at Russwood Park, in July 1956. When Elvis first appeared, dressed all in black except for red socks and tie, the fans rushed out of their seats and swept forwards towards the stage. The last few months had given Elvis a new confidence, so he was able to tease and control the crowd without letting anything get out of hand.

Time out for Mum and Dad

Top: Elvis takes time out to have a few words with his mother, Gladys, and father, Vernon. *Bottom*: The Colonel always had a supply of photographs for the fans to buy – and Elvis was happy to sign them. In later years, he rarely went out in public because he was constantly mobbed by his fans.

Hollywood, here I come

In August 1956, filming began on Elvis's first movie, *Love Me Tender*, which was being made by Twentieth-Century Fox. After his screen test for Hal Wallis, Elvis had been offered a three-picture deal by Paramount – but they had no suitable vehicle for him, so had loaned him to Twentieth-Century Fox. Elvis had an excellent memory, and he not only knew his own part before he arrived in Hollywood, but had also learned the entire script by heart. His co-stars were Richard Egan and Debra Paget, both experienced actors, and Elvis was very nervous but also extremely willing to learn. The producer, David Weisbart, had produced *Rebel Without a Cause* and Elvis was excited to meet him as he had deeply admired James Dean.

Down on the farm...

Originally entitled *The Reno Brothers, Love Me Tender* was a drama, set just after the Civil War. Elvis played the youngest son of a farming family, who marries the girlfriend of his eldest brother after everyone assumes that the brother is dead. When the older brother returns, the family is torn apart and Elvis's character is killed. Since the producers worried that the fans would be upset if their idol died, an alternative ending was shot, in which he survives. In the end they stayed with the original storyline, but Elvis appears again at the end, singing the title song over the credits.

Love Me Tender: a million orders

The theme song, 'Love Me Tender', was based on a Civil War ballad called 'Aura Lee'. Elvis was better known for more raunchy numbers, but he sang the ballad with real feeling. When it was released in September 1956 as a single the song was a great hit, so the name of the film was quickly changed to *Love Me Tender* before it was released. This was the only movie in which Elvis appeared where the part was not specifically written for him – in fact Robert Wagner was originally under consideration to play the role.

Time revealed that RCA had record-breaking advance orders of one million for the single, and even before the film opened the record reached No. 1 in the *Billboard* Top 100.

Natural acting ability

Producer David Weisbart told reporters that Elvis had the same smoldering appeal for teenagers, and the same impulsive nature, as James Dean. He advised Elvis not to have acting lessons but to rely on his greatest asset – his natural ability.

Opposite top: Debra Paget played the elder brother's girlfriend in *Love Me Tender*. Elvis had a big crush on her, but she did not return his regard – although she thought he was 'very sweet'.

Opposite bottom: Although *Love Me Tender* had only four musical numbers, they were carefully worked into the storyline.

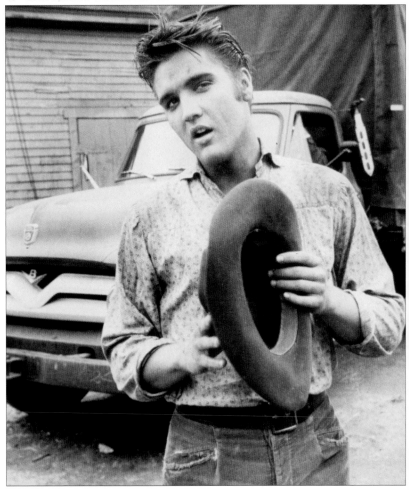

Charming the birds from the trees…

Elvis was well-liked by his co-stars, and they went out of their way to help him in the new and strange world of movie-making. Richard Egan, who played the elder brother, said of him later, 'That boy could charm the birds from the trees'.

Director Robert Webb was very patient with his fledgling star, taking him aside between shots to go over the scenes and breaking the lines down to show the emphasis.

Back home in Tupelo

Nick Adams, an actor and Hollywood hustler who had become Elvis's friend, introduced him to Natalie Wood. The papers reported that Elvis and Natalie were having a sizzling romance, but they usually went around in a gang with Nick and his other friends. Natalie described Elvis as 'a real pixie… he has a wonderful little-boy quality'.

Opposite: In September, Elvis appeared at a homecoming concert back in Tupelo. Before the concert began a parade was held in his honour, but the Colonel vetoed the suggestion that Elvis should ride in it because of concerns over security. Main Street was decked with a giant banner that said, 'Tupelo Welcomes Elvis Presley Home'. Elvis's parents, Vernon and Gladys, were there to see his triumph – though Gladys later told a friend that it had made her uncomfortable to remember how poor they had been when they lived there.

He wore Blue Velvet

For the concert, Elvis wore a heavy blue velvet shirt that Natalie Wood had had made for him by her own tailor – despite the fact that it was a very hot day. He teased the crowd, walking close to the edge of the stage and leaning down so the fans could just touch his fingers. One time he misjudged the distance, and lost one of the silver buttons from his shirt.

During the concert, Tupelo mayor James Ballard gave Elvis the key to the city and Mississippi governor JP Coleman came on stage to praise 'America's number-one entertainer'.

On second thoughts…

Ed Sullivan discusses a few points with Elvis during preparations for his second appearance on *The Ed Sullivan Show* in October 1956. Although Sullivan had declared that Elvis would never appear on his show, he later backed down and signed him for three performances. Elvis was paid a total of $50,000 for his appearances – which was considerably more than the sum the Colonel had originally asked for when he first approached Sullivan and had been turned down. When the first show was broadcast in early September, actor Charles Laughton acted as host since Sullivan was recovering from a car accident.

Fooling with Bill Black

While Elvis played to the girls, Bill Black often played the fool with his bass in the background. Sometimes he pretended to dance with it, at others he rode it like horse – which always elicited a laugh from the audience. The ratings for the *Sullivan Show* – and every other show – invariably went up when Elvis appeared.

Hear no evil…

Rehearsing for *The Ed Sullivan Show*. By this time Elvis appeared relaxed and confident.
Opposite: Despite all the controversy, Elvis enjoyed appearing before an audience, along with
Scotty Moore, DJ Fontana on drums, and Bill Black on bass. At the end of Elvis's third
appearance on his show, Ed Sullivan told the audience that he thought Elvis was 'a real decent
fine boy'.

Star guest

Liberace talking to Elvis in the audience on the opening night of his concert at the Hotel Riviera in Las Vegas. Elvis was taking a few days off in Vegas, staying at the New Frontier Hotel.
Opposite: Elvis and June Juanico, whom he had first met in her home town of Biloxi when he had played the Keesler Air Force Base in 1955. Almost a year later they met again in Memphis and dated for several months through the summer of 1956.

Just pure gold

After the concert, Liberace and Elvis swapped jackets and instruments and fooled around for the cameras. Liberace's jacket was a gold cutaway, and was the inspiration for the famous $2,500 gold-lamé suit that the Colonel had made up for Elvis by Nudie Cohen the following year. Liberace told journalists, 'Elvis and I may be characters – but we can afford to be.' Elvis always sent flowers for Liberace's opening nights.

November 1956

When *Love Me Tender* was released in November 1956, a huge cut-out of Elvis as Clint Reno was unveiled on a New York City cinema. Thousands of fans turned out to see the film – despite the fact that the critics' reviews of Elvis's performance were derisive and condescending. The reviews were hardly surprising, given the bad publicity Elvis had been getting throughout the year, but they were very unfair. For an inexperienced actor, Elvis acquitted himself very well.

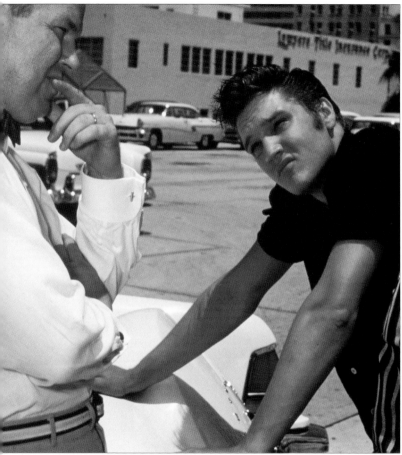

A casual, windswept Elvis. By the end of 1956, he had come a long way. His records were now in the charts, he had a nationwide following of fans and had made his first Hollywood movie, which was a big box office success. Despite all the adulation, most people agree that in terms of his character he had changed very little. He was still unfailingly polite and charming to everyone he met, and he still went home to his parents whenever he had the opportunity. However, the obsessive behaviour of the fans was becoming an increasing problem – Elvis could hardly walk down the street without being besieged by adoring admirers.

Car-crazy…

Below: The former truck driver studies the engine of something a little more powerful. Throughout his life Elvis had a fascination for cars and he not only bought many for himself, he also often bought them as gifts for friends, acquaintances – and even total strangers. The first car he ever owned was a 1941 Lincoln coupé, bought by Vernon and Gladys. When he first began to earn serious money he bought his mother a brand new pink Cadillac – even though she did not drive.

Left: A relaxed Elvis in front of the camera.

The sign on the wall reads:

...NITENTIARY

PERSONEL

...ON	1
...EP WDN	4
CAPT	9
CO	244
CMLIAN	165
TOTAL	421

INMATE

PEN	2680
ADDL	186
TRIAL	42

PEN	2889
DORM	198
TOTAL	3082

CHAPTER TWO

Treat Me Nice

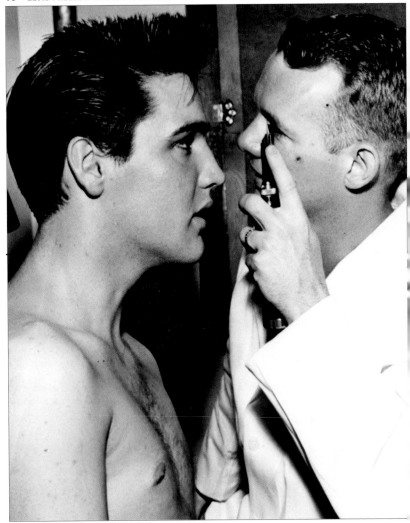

Dr Fred Jeff Burford, of St Petersburg, Florida, gives Elvis his pre-induction physical. Dr Burford gave the final OK that made Elvis eligible for the draft.

By the beginning of 1957, Elvis was accompanied by armed security guards wherever he went, since he could no longer step into the street without being mobbed by fans, causing a riot. He was constantly surrounded by members of his entourage, a close-knit circle of men who were both companions and support group. They rushed to fulfil his every whim, and were on hand 24 hours a day to sing gospel or to party. Sometimes badly behaved, they appeared arrogant to outsiders, and they became known as the 'Memphis Mafia'.

After Elvis had played a concert, he and the Mafia would usually party all night with local musicians – and plenty of girls, too. To relax, he sang gospel music or played the piano. He could now afford to buy whatever he wanted to eat, but had a weakness for junk food, particularly cheeseburgers, sliced banana and peanut butter sandwiches, greasy doughnuts, crispy burnt bacon, fried or mashed potatoes and dark-brown gravy. A diet of this kind was beginning to cause weight problems – although he was still burning off a great many calories in nervous energy. He also often walked in his sleep when he was anxious or upset, which gave those around him cause for concern about his safety. During the unhappy booking in 1956 at the New Frontier Hotel in Las Vegas, his companion Red West regularly sat up all night in case Elvis walked straight out of the open window.

Despite Elvis's burgeoning health problems, the hours spent on the road, the constant lack of sleep and his poor diet, he always seemed to find plenty of energy when it was time to take the stage.

For some time, rumours had been spreading that Elvis was about to be drafted. Early in 1957, he reported to the Kennedy Veterans Hospital in Memphis for his pre-induction US Army physical. He was classed 1-A and therefore eligible for military service, although the authorities said it was unlikely he would be called within the next six months. The Army also confirmed that the famous hair – Elvis's pride and joy – would have to come off. Meanwhile, there was another film to be made, *Loving You*, about a singer in search of fame. It also starred Lizbeth Scott and Wendell Corey – established actors who would not feel the need to eclipse the new kid on the block. Gladys and Vernon came to visit their son on-set and were filmed for one scene, watching the concert that takes place at the climax of the story.

One of the first major purchases Elvis made with his new-found wealth was a home for his parents, in Audubon Drive, Memphis. Unfortunately, fans often turned up in their hundreds to hang around outside, and the neighbours soon tired of this constant intrusion. Elvis decided he needed a property with some seclusion, so Vernon and Gladys set out to find one. As soon as they saw Graceland they fell in love with it, and quickly called Elvis to come and see it for himself. A Georgian colonial-style mansion, Graceland had been built in 1939 for Dr Thomas Moore and his wife, and named after Mrs Moore's great aunt Grace, who had owned the land. It was set in 13.75 acres of grounds, and placed well back from Highway 51 – later to be renamed Elvis Presley Boulevard. Elvis was immediately enthusiastic about the property, and the purchase was completed within a week. Renovations were soon under way, as well as essential structural repairs. Elvis had a swimming pool added, and installed a real soda fountain and specially made gates with a musical note motif. He had the interior entirely redecorated, mostly in dark colours with glitzy touches. Over the years, further additions included a recording studio, a 40-foot trophy room, stables, fenced-in fields and vegetable gardens.

His mother was very happy at the idea of moving in and wanted her own chicken house and hog pen, but things did not turn out quite the way she expected. She soon missed the company and the casual get-togethers that had been a major part of her life in town, and began to feel increasingly isolated. Elvis was constantly touring or filming, and Vernon seemed to be busy much of the time. Even when Elvis was there, he was surrounded by other people, as Graceland had also become home to various members of the Memphis Mafia and to a changing population of band members, back-up singers and starlets. This meant that Gladys had little time alone with her son.

Although Elvis continued to perform regularly, it was becoming somewhat hazardous to attend his concerts because of the wild behaviour of some of the fans –

and even he couldn't hear himself sing over the noise they made. There was also growing discontent in his backing group, as Bill Black, Scotty Moore and drummer DJ Fontana were still only being paid a flat rate of $200 a week when they were working, with a retainer of $100 a week when they were not. Since they were by no means working full-time but, at the same time, were banned from appearing other than with Elvis, their incomes were severely limited. DJ had come in later than the others and had always been a salaried employee so he was relatively content, but the Blue Moon Boys had been with Elvis from the beginning and felt they deserved better. Apart from the money problem, they were bored in Hollywood, where they had little to do, and found they were increasingly being excluded from direct contact with Elvis himself.

Above: Las Vegas dancer Dorothy Harmony accompanied Elvis to his pre-induction physical in February 1958. He had met Dorothy during his first appearance in Vegas the previous year and they had been dating regularly since. She had spent two weeks with the Presley family in Memphis over Christmas and the photographs of her opening her presents with the family precipitated his split with June Juanico.

Shooting was soon to begin on another film, *Jailhouse Rock*, in which Elvis plays a bad boy who reforms in prison and goes on to become a famous singing star. It was one of his best movies, with specially commissioned songs by Leiber and Stoller, who came out to Hollywood to oversee the recording. Unfortunately, one of the Colonel's stipulations in his management of Elvis was to make sure that the writers of his songs handed over a percentage of their royalties. Word of this soon got around, seriously limiting the selection of songs Elvis was offered in later years – to the point that it began to damage his career.

During rehearsals for the opening dance sequence in *Jailhouse Rock*, a porcelain cap came off one of Elvis's teeth and he managed to inhale it. The cap lodged in one of his lungs and he was taken to the hospital, where doctors retrieved it by inserting an instrument via his vocal cords and down into the lung. Elvis was hoarse for a few days afterwards, but to everyone's relief, his voice soon recovered.

Elvis got along very well with Judy Tyler, his co-star in *Jailhouse Rock*, but, being newly married, she wasn't interested in any sort of romantic attachment with him. Tragically, she and her husband were killed in a car accident soon after filming finished, and Elvis was so upset he could never watch the finished picture. Another important relationship hit the rocks in this period. The DJ Dewey Phillips, who had first played 'That's All Right, Mama' and been so instrumental in launching Elvis's career, came out to visit him in Hollywood. Elvis played him a single that was about to be released, 'Teddy Bear', from his previous film, *Loving You*. Phillips loved it and, against Elvis's explicit instructions, took a copy of the record and played it on air on his return to Memphis. Because the record had not even been released, Phillips' scoop infuriated both the Colonel and record executives, and Elvis and Phillips had a major falling-out. Although they were later to patch things up, their friendship was never quite the same.

Back in Memphis, Elvis began dating Anita Wood, a blonde former beauty queen whom he had first seen on the television show *Top Ten Dance Party*, broadcast on WHBQ. Although he continued to see other women throughout their relationship, the romance was fairly serious; she was a regular visitor to Graceland and got along very well with Elvis's mother. He gave Anita a sapphire and diamond ring, which she publicly told reporters was merely a friendship ring – although she and many others believed privately that it was meant as much more.

At the same time, Gladys herself was not only depressed, but was becoming increasingly unwell – she had a liver problem and suffered badly from fluid retention, so her ankles and legs often swelled. It was not like her to complain about her problems, but according to several members of the Memphis Mafia, it was around this period that she began to drink heavily and in secret.

By September 1957, Scotty Moore and Bill Black decided they had accepted poor salaries and bad treatment for long enough. There seemed no sign of any imminent change, so they both resigned. They had played a large part in Elvis's success, but felt that he had not shared it with them – while he had become wealthy, they were in debt. Elvis made a belated offer of more money, but it was too little too late as, in the meantime, the newspapers had seized on the story and run an interview with both musicians. Elvis felt betrayed, and immediately began auditioning new backing players. Although he found two good musicians, it just wasn't the same, and after a while, both sides swallowed their pride and Scotty and Bill came back – but only for an improved daily rate.

Elvis was scheduled to begin work on his fourth film, *King Creole*, at the end of December, but in the middle of that month he finally received his draft notice. Previously, representatives from the military authorities had offered him special status: the Navy planned to form a company around him that would entertain the troops; the Air Force suggested he could spend his time touring recruiting centres. Elvis turned down their offers, saying that he just wanted to be treated like any other soldier – he was aware that any sign that he was being treated differently would be reported in the press and cause a great deal of resentment. Publicly he announced that he was happy to go and do his duty, to give back a little in return for what America had done for him. Privately, though, he was very worried, and told friends that he feared a long absence might cause fans to forget him. He did not have to leave immediately, however; on behalf of Paramount he requested a 60-day deferment to allow him to film *King Creole*, pointing out that, unless he did so, the studio would lose the large sum of money it had already spent on pre-production. The request was granted, and filming began.

By now, Elvis was earning a fortune – although no one will ever know exactly how much. Even Elvis himself had no idea how much the Colonel received for any of his performances or movies; he wasn't interested in the business details. As long as the promises the Colonel made to him were kept, in a professional capacity he was content to be where he was supposed to be and do what he was told to do. As well as the management contract with Elvis, the recording deals, the music publishing, and the film contracts – all of which certainly gave the Colonel more than his fair share – many people suspect that he also took millions of dollars on the side that neither Elvis nor the IRS knew about. He always had promotional items on sale outside concerts and the hotels where Elvis was staying, and was quick to come up with new gimmicks if he thought the fans would buy them. Now 'his boy' was going into the Army and would not be available for two years. The Colonel was nothing if not resourceful, however, and would soon come up with a way to turn the situation to his advantage.

Art follows life…

The storyline of Elvis's second film, *Loving You*, was loosely based on his own life. Elvis played Deke Rivers, an unknown but talented singer with a new sound. Lizabeth Scott, a hard-headed music promoter, exploits him for his appeal to teenage audiences but the press soon label him as a bad influence and a rebel. After Deke manages to convince people that he is really a fine, upstanding young man, the movie ends happily.

Opposite top: Although here it is in pristine condition, Elvis's cars were often defaced by his female fans, who were so desperate to meet him that they wrote their telephone numbers and messages in lipstick all over the paint work.

Opposite bottom: Gladys and Vernon are pictured with just a few of the hundreds of gifts from fans that Elvis received on his 22nd birthday. The fans often gathered outside his parents' home in Memphis and the neighbours were beginning to get annoyed with the constant intrusions.

Proud owner of Graceland

Opposite: The new owner of Graceland stands proudly next to one of the columns of the entrance portico. The renovations and decorations that Elvis wanted were to cost almost as much again as the house itself – and one of his priorities was to create 'the most beautiful bedroom in Memphis' for his mother.

Above: One of the new additions Elvis made to Graceland was the installation of a pair of custom-made gates with a musical motif.

In trouble...

Above: Elvis got himself into trouble when he was accused of pulling a gun on a Private First Class Hershel, after the young Marine claimed Elvis had insulted his wife. Since Elvis had never met Mrs Hershel – and the gun was a prop, which he had brought back from Hollywood – the whole affair was settled out of court.

Opposite; Jailhouse Rock was a low-budget movie shot in black and white, with stylized sets, but the simple settings enhanced the serious storyline. Many believe it was one of the best films Elvis ever made – and it made a great deal of money for MGM and for Elvis himself, who received a large percentage of the profits.

1957: Jailhouse Rock

In *Jailhouse Rock* Elvis plays Vince Everett, who is sent to prison for killing a man in self-defence. His character is hot-blooded and bitter over the unfair sentence, and becomes an angry, sullen and brooding young man. The fans are therefore treated to several scenes of a very passionate and provocative Elvis.

For the big dance sequence performed to the title song, Elvis was backed by a team of professional dancers. He had initially been wary about the whole idea, but choreographer Alex Romero watched Elvis move around naturally when he was singing, and then worked the steps up into a routine. Elvis was much more comfortable and enthusiastic with the final result, and it looks very like the way he normally moved on stage. The single 'Jailhouse Rock'/'Treat Me Nice' was also a great success and sold over three million copies in 12 months in the US. It was the first Elvis record to reach No. 1 in the charts in Britain.

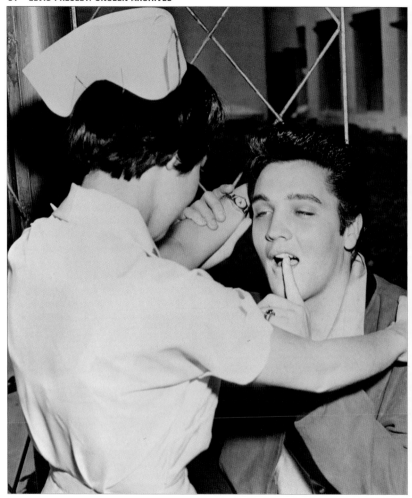

Elvis threw himself into the dance routine with such abandon that he swallowed one of the temporary caps from his teeth. It lodged in his lung and had to be recovered with surgery. For a while there was some concern that Elvis's voice would be affected, but the fears proved to be groundless.

Bad boy image

Top: Jailhouse Rock played on Elvis's bad boy image. While Vince Everett is in jail, he learns to sing and play the guitar from another inmate. Afterwards Vince becomes a famous rock star, but is not a particularly pleasant person until an accident stops him in his tracks. He becomes a nice guy who falls in love with the heroine, Peggy van Alden, played by Judy Tyler.

Bottom: Elvis and Anne Neyland, a former Miss Texas who also appeared in *Jailhouse Rock,* exchange a smoldering look. They dated during the shooting of the movie and for a few weeks afterwards.

True love in the movies

Judy Tyler, as Peggy van Alden, watches Vince during one of the scenes from
Jailhouse Rock. Peggy is the record promoter who helps Vince to stardom and falls in
love with him – but haughtily refuses to respond to his advances until he becomes a
reformed man.

Devastated by Judy's death

Elvis and Judy were great friends during the shooting of the movie – but Judy was
newly married and not interested in romance. A few weeks after shooting finished,
she and her husband were killed in a car accident. Elvis was devastated and did not
attend the film's premiere.

Star of stage and screen...

Right: While he was filming *Jailhouse Rock*, Elvis was assigned the Clark Gable dressing room. When he and his entourage appeared on the set for the first time, all the office workers poured out to see him – causing serious security problems. Elvis enjoyed working in Hollywood and being surrounded by people in show business, and he soon made a lot of friends there.

Below: When *Jailhouse Rock* was released, the fans were ecstatic. It went on to make a profit within only three weeks.

Opposite: Actress Venetia Stevenson was the daughter of Anna Lee and director Robert Stevenson. She and Elvis dated on and off through 1957 and 1958, but their relationship was never serious.

Parting is such sweet sorrow...

Anita Wood hugs Elvis goodbye, as he prepares to leave on a whirlwind tour of the Pacific northwest. Anita was a former beauty queen, who was now appearing on *Top Ten Dance Party* on WHBQ. She had just won the Mid-South Hollywood Star Hunt and was also about to leave, for the finalists' competition in New Orleans. The two of them were together for several years – although that didn't stop Elvis from dating a number of other women during the same period.

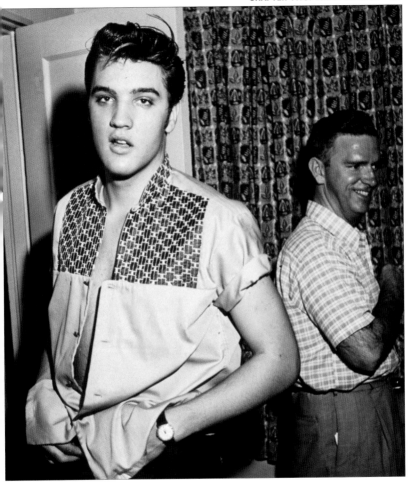

Elvis's tour…

The tour covered five cities in four days, so there was little time for rest and relaxation.
Elvis and Tom Diskin, his road manager, were accompanied by George Klein, Lamar Fike and
Cliff Gleaves. By this stage, Elvis had a string of hits including 'All Shook Up', 'Teddy Bear'
and 'Jailhouse Rock' which were all released during 1957.

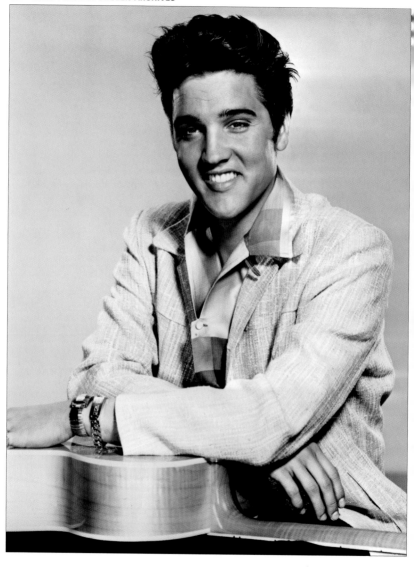

Causing a riot on tour

During the tour there were riots in nearly every city, and in Spokane, Washington, fans broke onto the infield of the Memorial Stadium and tried to steal the soil because Elvis's feet had touched it. In Vancouver, a contingent of Canadian Mounties had been drafted in to hold back the crowd of 25,000, but they were quickly overwhelmed. The Colonel pulled Elvis offstage and the fans were told to get back to their seats before he would continue. Elvis couldn't resist teasing the crowd again, and the concert was stopped for a second time. Finally they managed to proceed, but at the end Elvis was whisked away as fans engulfed the stage, grabbing everything they could get their hands on.

Above: Elvis studies his reviews. He now ended every show with 'Hound Dog', which he introduced as the 'Elvis Presley national anthem'. After the tour was over he was scheduled to go on to a recording session organized by RCA, to lay down tracks for a special Christmas album.

A professional touch…

During the filming of *Jailhouse Rock* Elvis became friendly with professional dancer Russ Tamblyn, who gave him a few tips to sharpen up his dancing style.

ELVIS
IN
ACTION
AS
NEVER
BEFORE!

Millionaire mover with MGM deal

After *Jailhouse Rock* was released nationwide, the Colonel estimated that he and Elvis were due to make more than two million dollars through their percentage deal with MGM.

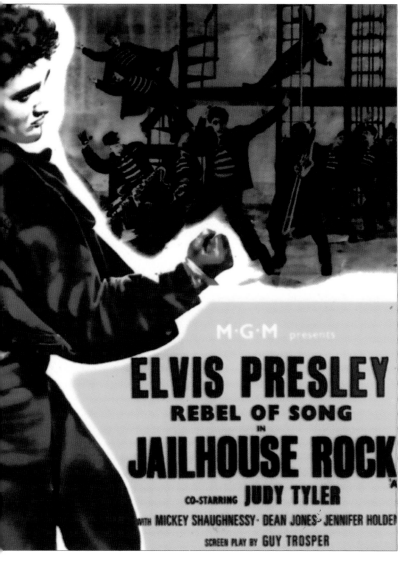

Screaming and swooning

The fans now made so much noise during the concerts that no one could hear Elvis sing. They even screamed and swooned while just watching him on the screen.

Below: The Memphis premiere of *Jailhouse Rock* was held in the cinema where Elvis had once worked briefly as an usher.

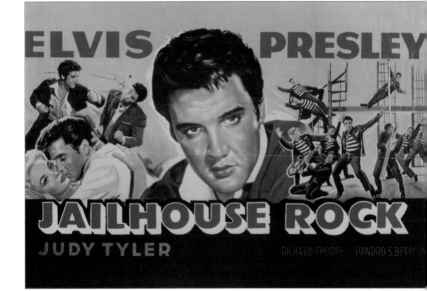

Drafted!

Just before Christmas 1957, Elvis received his draft notification and although he collected the notice himself to avoid publicity, the press soon got wind of it. He told reporters that he was happy the situation was finally resolved and that he was happy to return something to the country that had given him so much. When photographers wanted to picture him with the notice a minor panic ensued, as Elvis couldn't remember where he had put it.

CHAPTER THREE

It's Now or Never

A brooding Elvis throws a punch for the benefit of photographers.

Early in January 1958, Elvis flew to California to record the soundtrack for *King Creole* and then begin filming. The movie told the story of a young man who dropped out of college and became involved with gangsters, but then overcame adversity to become a famous singer. It had some similarities with Elvis's life and was one of the few of his own films that he liked. Both the director, Michael Curtiz, and Elvis's co-star, Walter Matthau (who played the heavy), were impressed with how Elvis approached the role, and believed he would go on to become a great actor. Elvis himself was determined to do his best, as it might be his last film. Who knew what would happen when he returned from the Army?

Two weeks after shooting had finished, Elvis was finally inducted into the US Army. He arrived early at the draft board, accompanied by Anita Wood and various friends and relatives, to be greeted by the Colonel and a group of journalists and photographers from the press. After a short media interview, Elvis was taken off to the Kennedy Veterans Hospital with his fellow recruits to be checked out, but even his medical examination was conducted in the glare of publicity. The bus taking Elvis on to Fort Chaffee, Arkansas, was followed by hundreds of cars and, at a scheduled stop for coffee and sandwiches, there were so many people already waiting that no one was able to leave the bus. The commander in charge at Fort Chaffee had agreed that the press would have full access, so Elvis made his bed for the cameras, had breakfast with the Colonel and newsmen, and was photographed having his hair cut, and being issued with and wearing his uniform. He was assigned to the Second Armored Division at Fort Hood in Texas for basic training, where he was also to receive advanced tank instruction. Having seen the circus around Fort Chaffee, those in charge at Fort Hood decided to take a different approach. The media were given one day of free access, after which the new recruit was strictly off-limits. It was the first time Elvis had been on his own, away from his family and friends. Although he was homesick, he kept his feelings to himself and buckled down to learning how to be a soldier. After some initial difficulties, the other soldiers eventually accepted him as one of the boys.

The Colonel discovered that a soldier could live off base after basic training if he had dependants in the area. So Vernon and Gladys quickly packed up and moved to Killeen, the nearest town to the base. At first they lived in a trailer, but since Vernon's mother, Minnie Presley, and one of the Memphis Mafia, Lamar Fike, had come with them, they soon found a house to rent instead. Elvis drove back and forth to the base each day, and at weekends Anita often came to stay.

Everything seemed to be progressing smoothly, but Gladys was feeling increasingly ill and the hot Texas summer wasn't helping. In August she decided to return to Memphis to see her doctor, who rushed her off to hospital. Despite many tests it was unclear exactly what the problem was, but it was certainly serious and Elvis was called. He was initially unable to get leave, but after threatening to go AWOL, was given a pass on compassionate grounds. Although she appeared to rally when Elvis appeared, Gladys died of a heart attack two days later.

Elvis was inconsolable, and not embarrassed to show it. He and his father wept openly, and Elvis told the press that his mother's death had broken his heart. They had been so close, despite the time they had spent apart over the last few years while he had been building his career; she had been the one person he could always trust to be there for him. Her body was laid out at Graceland so that friends and relatives could pay their last respects. Elvis couldn't stop touching her, patting her hands, kissing her and pleading with her to come back. Those close to him eventually talked him away and he was given a sedative to help him sleep. At the funeral, Elvis almost collapsed, and old friends rallied round to help him get through the next few days, but just over a week after his mother's death he had to return to Fort Hood and the Army.

There were several more weeks of training to get through, and Elvis was a diligent recruit and managed well despite his grief. The following month, his unit was transferred by train to New York, where it was to join the ship that would take it to Germany. Elvis's embarkation was marked by the usual media circus – at a press conference he answered questions about the Army, marriage, his mother and his music, and was photographed going up the gangplank with a borrowed duffel bag. Elvis was not going abroad alone, though – he had arranged for Vernon, his grandmother, and Memphis Mafia members Lamar Fike and Red West to come over separately and set up home near his base. The Colonel was to stay behind in America to make sure 'his boy' was not forgotten while he was away.

Although he had never been abroad before – let alone toured there – Elvis was greeted by thousands of ecstatic fans when his ship docked at Bremerhaven. His unit transferred by train to Friedberg, where he was to spend his service, and after a press conference in the canteen, all media were banned from the US base. A day later, Elvis's entourage arrived in the country, and after renting rooms in a couple of hotels for several months, settled in a rented house at Goethestrasse 14, which became Elvis's home when he was not on duty for the rest of the time he was in Germany.

Although Elvis did the usual soldier's duties and went on manoeuvres while in the Army, he had an easier life than many soldiers. Lamar and Red looked after his uniform for him, and he had enough money to buy spare kit, so he always looked smart. During several of his leaves, he and his friends travelled to Paris, where they visited famous nightclubs such as the Folies Bergère, the Lido and the Moulin Rouge, and the showgirls were always ready to party.

Elvis dated several German girls while he was in their country, but there were no serious relationships. He was still seeing Anita, and she came over to visit him several times. However, at a club in Wiesbaden in November 1959, he was introduced to Priscilla Beaulieu. The step-daughter of an Army officer, Priscilla was only 14, but very pretty and Elvis enjoyed her company. They saw each other regularly during the rest of the time he was there, and he met her parents, but since he was also still seeing other women, their relationship was by no means exclusive. Vernon also met someone – Dee Stanley, the wife of a sergeant and mother of three young boys. She and Vernon soon began an affair, which deeply upset Elvis since it was only just over a year since his beloved mother had died.

Meanwhile the Colonel was keeping things going in America. Before he left, Elvis had recorded several songs, so there were still some records to release in his absence. The Colonel also made sure there was a steady stream of stories in the press about Elvis and his Army career – complete with a few pictures of him looking handsome in uniform. He sent out messages on Elvis's behalf and made sure the fans were kept satisfied; although he was careful not to flood the market so that they would still want more. He was so successful that more than one million advance orders for any record Elvis cared to make on his return had already been received, and several new film projects were agreed.

In March 1960, after two years, Elvis's Army career was finally drawing to a close. He had been promoted twice, and now held the rank of sergeant – although pictures taken on his return show his uniform with an extra stripe, denoting the rank of staff sergeant, which he did not earn. Before he left Germany, Priscilla came to bid him a tearful farewell and he promised to call her, but she was not certain she would ever see him again. Back in America, as he went through the motions of being discharged, the media circus began to gear up again, with coverage of him receiving his final pay cheque – and immediately handing it over to the Colonel – waving to crowds in his uniform, and the journey back home to Graceland.

Most people agree that his time in the service changed Elvis – afterwards he was more mature and conservative professionally, and his music became more mainstream. However, there was also another and more serious change. According to several people who knew him at the time, Elvis had started to take amphetamines regularly. Apparently, he had first used them to help him stay awake during night manoeuvres in Germany, but now took them on a daily basis – not only to keep him going but to help him stay thin. He had come out of the Army 15 pounds lighter than when he went in, but still tended to prefer junk food. Throughout his life, he strongly disapproved of drug-taking, but since the amphetamines were prescription drugs, he did not regard them in the same light. The pills not only caused unpredictable mood swings, but also contributed to Elvis's growing disconnection from the normal world.

One of the first things the Colonel had lined up for his return was an appearance on a Frank Sinatra special, which was to be taped at the Fountainbleau Hotel in Miami Beach. Elvis caught a train down to Florida, and the track was lined with people for almost its entire length – his fans had not forgotten him. After the show, he went back to the studio to record new songs, and then to begin the soundtrack for a new film, *GI Blues*. The movie's storyline was lightweight and capitalized on Elvis's time in the Army. His character was a soldier who also happens to be a musician, who falls in love with a cabaret singer. It was set in Germany, but all of Elvis's scenes were shot in Hollywood. It marked a change from his previous films in that he was no longer playing a bad boy who makes good, but a safe and wholesome character. He also completed another western, *Flaming Star*, in 1960, and began shooting *Wild in the Country*, both for Twentieth Century Fox. These films allowed him to move away from his singing a little and tackle slightly more dramatic roles.

The Sinatra show was broadcast in May 1960, and the audience was split between those who loved Elvis's new, mature, laid-back style, and those who wondered where the rebel rocker had gone. The doubters were heavily outnumbered, though. Elvis lost few fans and picked up many more, so he was still one of the most popular singers in America.

At home, however, things were not so happy. Dee had divorced her former husband, and she and Vernon finally got married, although Elvis refused to go to their wedding. The newlyweds moved into Graceland with Dee's three sons for a while, but soon moved out again into a place of their own.

As he settled back into his old life, Elvis was still dating Anita, but he was also seeing several other women on a casual basis. Despite her doubts, he did call Priscilla regularly, and they talked about her coming over to America to see him. It was not to happen for another two years.

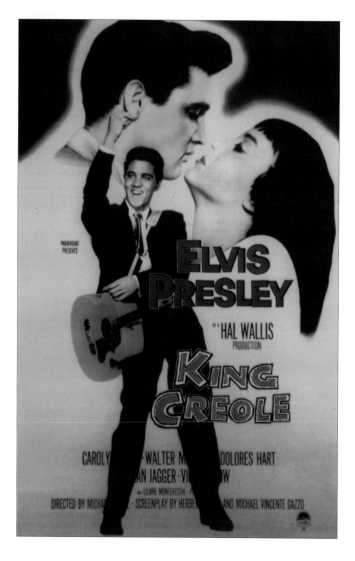

March 1958: You're in the Army now...

Above: Major Elbert P Turner swears Elvis into the Army at the draft board in Memphis, Tennessee. The new recruit told reporters that he was dreading the haircut he would get the following day, but that he hoped he would be treated the same as everyone else.

Opposite: Elvis's induction into the Army had been deferred so he could complete filming on *King Creole*. The story was of a young singer, Danny Fisher – played by Elvis – who is offered a job by a local mobster – played by Walter Matthau. Danny is a great success – but things go badly wrong when he becomes romantically involved with the mobster's girlfriend. With top production values and respected director Michael Curtiz, the movie earned Elvis his best reviews so far. The soundtrack for *King Creole* included two of Elvis's legendary songs, 'Hard Headed Woman' and 'Trouble'.

Leaving Memphis

Opposite: As the bus leaves Memphis for Fort Chaffee, Arkansas, a sad group of women watch Elvis go – including his current girlfriend, Anita Wood (centre). Press from around the world are on hand to record the entire proceedings and they follow the bus as it sets off.

Above: Many of Elvis's loyal female fans turn up to tell him they will not forget him while he is away, and Elvis happily chats to them and signs autographs. The press are constantly present with the Army's permission – although when one photographer hides in the barracks at Fort Chaffee to try to get a picture of Elvis sleeping in his bunk, it is decided that things have gone too far and the hapless snapper is thrown out.

Hair today

Elvis runs a comb through his trademark locks, which are due to be shorn the following day.
When he is issued with $7 in partial pay, the reporters ask what he will do with all the money,
and Elvis jokingly replies that he plans to start a loan company.

JAMES B. PETERSON
MANAGER

Gone tomorrow

There were 55 reporters and photographers on hand to record the famous haircut. Elvis held up some of the hair for the press, and joked, 'Hair today, gone tomorrow!'

Shot three times

The new-look Elvis faces the cameras. All the publicity surrounding the event got Elvis so flustered that he forgot to pay the barber his 65 cent fee, and had to be called back – much to his embarrassment.

Opposite: The Army shoots Elvis three times, when he gets his jabs for typhoid, tetanus and Asian flu. As well as medical tests and a haircut, he also had to do five hours of aptitude tests and sit through a two-hour lecture on a private's rights and privileges.

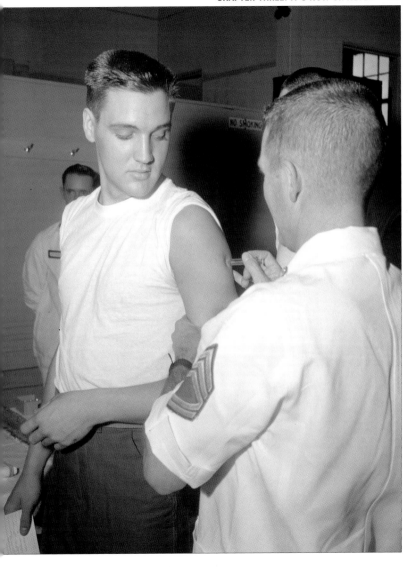

Fitted out for service

Opposite: Elvis tries on some snappy footwear and displays the latest design in Army fatigues. He dealt with all the press attention with great patience and good humour, only refusing to sign autographs while he was 'in ranks'.

It was soon announced that Elvis was to be assigned to the 2nd Armored Division at Fort Hood just outside Killeen in Texas, to do his basic training and advanced tank instruction. The 2nd Armored was General George Patton's famous 'Hell on Wheels' outfit. Six of the other Memphis draftees were also to be sent to Fort Hood, where basic training would last for eight weeks. There was no sign of the press attention letting up, so the Army was beginning to re-think its policy of full access.

Best-dressed soldier

As well as the Army fatigues, Elvis had been issued with a dress uniform. He later bought several spare sets of kit, which Memphis Mafia members Lamar Fike and Red West looked after for him when they were all in Germany. Elvis was always so well turned out that he won 'Best-Dressed Soldier' several times.

Elvis on leave

Above: Private Elvis Presley alights from the chartered Greyhound bus at Fort Hood in central Texas, after the day-long journey from Fort Chaffee in Arkansas. The bus had bypassed the usual stops in Dallas and Waxahachie, where hundreds of people had gathered. It finally stopped for lunch in Hillsboro, Texas, and two of the largest men were detailed to sit either side of Elvis. It was 25 minutes before anyone recognized him, but then a riot ensued as it took some time for everyone to get out of the building and back on the bus.

Left: On his first furlough in May 1958, Elvis returned to Graceland to see his family. He had 14 days leave, part of which was spent recording in Nashville so that RCA would have some new material to release while he was away.

A medal for sharpshooting…

Vernon Presley admires his son's medals. Elvis had earned his marksman medal with a carbine and his sharpshooter medal with a pistol and was now acting assistant squad leader. He told reporters that he had gradually been accepted by the others – he had never asked for anything and just did the same as everyone else.

Sneaking a preview

Left: During his leave, Elvis and his parents attended a sneak preview of *King Creole*, which was held in Memphis.

Below: Elvis was always happy to come down to the gates of Graceland to sign autographs and chat to the fans. When reporters asked him why he was wearing his uniform while on leave, he replied 'I'm kinda proud of it.' He also told them that he had adjusted to Army hours and was now having trouble staying awake after midnight.

Just visiting

Anita Wood smiles for photographers as she boards a plane to Texas. She was off to visit Elvis now he had returned to base. She stayed with Sergeant Norwood and his wife at their home on the base.

August 1958: Elvis mourns his mother

Above: In August 1958, Gladys Presley was admitted to hospital. The diagnosis was uncertain, but her illness was serious enough for Elvis to be given compassionate leave. He went straight to the hospital, where Vernon was already staying – sleeping in a folding cot next to the hospital bed. His visit seemed to cheer Gladys up and for a time the doctors thought she might recover. *Opposite:* In the early hours of Thursday morning Gladys died of a heart attack. When reporters arrived at Graceland later in the day, they found Vernon and Elvis sitting on the steps of the house. Elvis, sobbing uncontrollably, told them that his mother was all they had lived for and that she had always been his 'best girl'.

September '58: Off over the sea

Just over a week after the funeral Elvis had to return to Fort Hood to complete his basic training and a month later his unit left for Germany. Since 125 newsmen had arrived in New York to see him off, a press conference and photo opportunity were organized before he boarded the ship. His kit had already been loaded, so a borrowed duffel bag was quickly provided for the pictures. Although Elvis had never been in Europe, he already had fans there. At least 500 German teenagers arrived to welcome him when the ship docked at Bremerhaven. From the docks the soldiers caught a train to the base at Friedberg, near Frankfurt.

In Germany

Elvis poses in his dress uniform in Germany. At first he was hounded by photographers and bothered constantly by other soldiers looking for autographs, but the press were soon banned from the base and the other soldiers got used to his presence, so things settled down into a routine.

Margit dates her 'very nice boy'

Elvis holding hands with Margit Buergin, a young typist with an electrical supply company in Frankfurt. She had waited outside his hotel to get his autograph and photographers had called for them to kiss. Elvis happily obliged, and he dated Margit several times afterwards. She was only sixteen, but looked older, and still lived with her mother. She told the press that she thought Elvis was 'a very nice boy' and that she liked him very much.

Rocking with Bill Haley in Frankfurt

Bill Haley was appearing in Frankfurt on 23 October and in Stuttgart six days later. Elvis went to see him both times, although he had to stay backstage during the show to avoid causing a riot. He told Haley that he was grateful for his help and encouragement in the early days – and that, without it, he might still be driving a truck.

On maneuvers

Elvis was assigned to Company C, a scout platoon, where he drove a jeep for Reconnaissance Platoon Sergeant Ira Jones. One reason that Company C was selected was because it spent much of its time on manoeuvres, which would keep Private Presley well out of the public eye.

One of the boys

Elvis shaving at base camp in Grafenwöhr while on manoeuvres. It was a cold, dismal and muddy place near the border, but Elvis endured the same conditions as the other soldiers and turned out to be resourceful and clever scout. He proved himself not only to his platoon sergeant but also to his fellow soldiers and was finally accepted by them as one of the boys. While he was away, Vernon met Dee Stanley – who had been trying to persuade Elvis to come to dinner with her family – and the two of them became close. Dee later divorced her Army husband and married Vernon, much to Elvis's disapproval.

The day after Elvis returned from manoeuvres, he took possession of a second-hand white BMW 507 sports car that had previously been used by German racer Hans Stuck for demonstrations. At a photo call, the keys were handed over by a pretty model. He had also bought an old Cadillac for his father to use and a Volkswagen Beetle for the boys. The first Christmas in Germany was sad for everyone, not only because they were away from home but because it was the first without Gladys.

Opposite: Elvis demonstrates the equipment in his jeep to four-year-old Michael Jones, the son of his platoon sergeant, at an Open House held at the 3rd Armored Division headquarters in Friedberg in April 1959.

All teamwork but no touring

During the time he was in Germany, Elvis never once appeared on stage or sang for a proper audience. He had been instructed not to do so by Colonel Tom Parker – partly so that he would not be treated differently, but also partly because the Colonel did not see why the Army should get for free what everyone else was prepared to pay a fortune for. Back home, the Colonel was using Elvis's absence and the shortage of material to up the ante in all his negotiations with RCA and the Hollywood studios.

Above: When a World War I memorial in a German village had to be moved to a new location, the US Army stepped in to help. Private Presley directed operations as the sections were lifted by crane. Later he told the press that he thought he and the other soldiers had worked pretty well as a team.

Russia's public enemy number one

Elvis poses with an artillery gun. Russian leaders had dubbed him 'Public Enemy Number One' and accused the US of using him as a weapon in psychological warfare.

Promoted to acting sergeant

Elvis had already been promoted to the rank of Specialist Fourth Class, but in January 1960 he was promoted again to acting sergeant. He proudly shows off his new stripes to photographers.

Sergeant Presley is no richer

Opposite: The advancement in rank carried no increase in pay, but since Elvis was considerably richer than most soldiers, this did not concern him!

Above: While he was in Germany, Elvis did not live on base with the other soldiers. His family and a couple of the Memphis Mafia were there with him and at first they stayed in a series of hotels. After a shaving cream fight and an incident when a small fire set off all the alarms, they were asked to move out, so Elvis rented a house at Goethestrasse 14. Here his grandmother was able to cook the kind of food he liked – and Elvis was often able to slip back home for lunch.

Back in the field...

Sergeant Elvis Presley warms his hands by the camp fire. By this time he had been made up to full rank and his platoon were back out on manoeuvres at Grafenwöhr – and it was the middle of winter and bitterly cold. Elvis was looking forward to his discharge – he had only a couple more months to go.

Elvis and his fellow soldiers checking a map. He made several new friends in the Army, including Charlie Hodge who came to work for him in civilian life afterwards and stayed with Elvis right to the end.

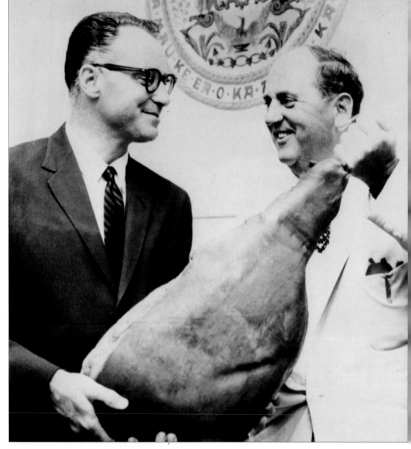

Colonel Parker holds the fort

The whole time Elvis was away, the Colonel kept his name in the public eye by judicious release of the material available. He also made sure the fan clubs were kept informed and sent out over four thousand telegrams and messages to fellow performers on his and Elvis's behalf. At a time when the industry was in a slump, he managed to keep Elvis on top. Here he gets a little extra publicity by presenting a whole ham to a state governor.

Elvis in Paris

The Army was not all mud and guns – here Elvis enjoys a few days R&R in Paris, where he stayed in the Prince de Galles in Avenue Georges V with Lamar Fike, Charlie Hodge and Rex Mansfield. They visited famous nightclubs such as the Moulin Rouge and the Folies Bergère and once took the entire chorus line of Bluebell girls from the Lido back to their hotel. They had so much fun in Paris that Elvis decided to stay one more night, paying for a limousine to drive them all back to Friedberg the following day.

Back to civilian life

Above: Donning his fatigues for the last time, Elvis studies himself in the mirror. He had survived two years in the Army and was now about to go home again. He told most of his Army buddies that he was looking forward to making more movies and hoped to do more serious roles – but to closer friends he confided that he was afraid the fans would have forgotten him.

Left: Elvis faces journalists at a last press conference in Germany in March 1960, before leaving for the US. He told newsmen that he had learned a lot from the Army and his commanding officer, General Richard J Brown, gave him a special certificate of merit for 'cheerfulness and drive and continually outstanding leadership ability'.

Goodbye

Priscilla Beaulieu waves goodbye as Elvis departs from Rhine-Main air base. When reporters asked about her, Elvis had said she was a 'nice girl' whom he had seen several times. Although he had promised to keep in touch, she was certain that she would never see him again.

A snowy homecoming

Sergeant Elvis Presley carries his bags through the snow, after arriving in New Jersey from Germany in March 1960. He was transferred to Fort Dix, where he stayed for 48 hours until he was officially discharged.

Opposite top: Back in Germany Priscilla is pictured with her photograph of Elvis as she writes him a letter. All the papers referred to her as his 16-year-old girlfriend, but at the time she was still only 14 – although she was very mature for her age. Her family had insisted on meeting Elvis before they would let her see him regularly, but were won over by his charm and sincerity.

Opposite bottom: The press were on hand again to record every step of the discharge proceedings. Here Elvis boards a bus at Fort Dix that will take him from his orientation lecture to the base finance building to collect his final pay.

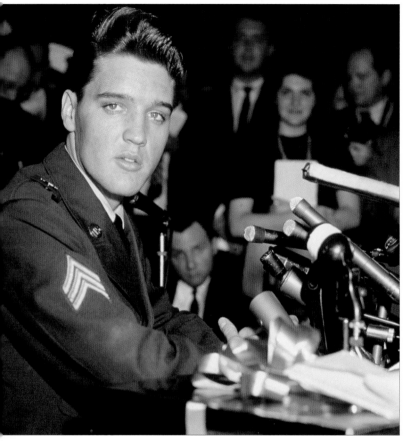

March 1960: Parker's 'boy' is back

Opposite: Colonel Parker looks on as Elvis waves to fans. He had carefully orchestrated all the details of the homecoming, making sure that the fans were around to give Elvis the kind of welcome he deserved – and prove once and for all that Elvis was still on top.

Above: At a press conference, Elvis wore a specially-tailored formal dress uniform – but the tailor had made a mistake with the stripes. The extra rocker on the shoulder designated a rank of staff sergeant, but Elvis had only made sergeant. Some reporters accepted it was a mistake – the more cynical blamed the Colonel for trying to build up the reputation of 'his boy'.

Back to work – and play

Above: Lucky fan Barbara Ann Murray of Roselle Park, New Jersey, gets to sit on Elvis's lap and receives a kiss.

Right: Actress Tina Louise, who went on to become the star of *Gilligan's Island*, interviews Elvis for the cameras.

Opposite: With his hair already beginning to grow out of the regulation Army haircut, Elvis was beginning to look more like the King of Rock 'n' Roll again. He told reporters that he planned to rest at home – although in fact he had a busy schedule. He not only had a recording session planned, but also an appearance on the *Frank Sinatra Show* and was soon to start shooting on a new movie. Instead he told the newsmen about his newfound interest in karate, which he had been studying in Germany.

Welcome home, Elvis

Also on hand to greet the homecoming star was Nancy Sinatra, who presented him with a gift from her father. They were soon linked romantically – although the relationship never appeared very serious on either side.

Opposite: After collecting an autograph, Barbara Ann Murray gives Elvis a welcome home hug.

March 1960: Official discharge

After being officially discharged, Elvis signs a few autographs for his Army buddies.
Opposite: Elvis shows the waiting newsmen his certificate of discharge and the contents of his
last pay packet.

Priscilla: the girl he left behind

Left: Priscilla consoles herself by playing Elvis records back in Germany. She was delighted when he did keep his promise to stay in touch, and soon he was making plans to bring her over to America.

Above: The Colonel reminds Elvis not to forget his commission – and Elvis hands him the entire $109.54.

Opposite: Elvis's appearance on the *Frank Sinatra Show* indicated a change of direction. Perfectly dressed and incredibly elegant in a tuxedo, he sang two songs with professional aplomb, and then did a duet with Sinatra himself. Although some fans mourned the passing of the hell-raising Elvis, most agreed that he had matured and loved the new style.

Elvis, we still love you!

On his train journey down to Miami to record the Sinatra show, almost the entire route was lined with fans and press. Of course the Colonel had taken the trouble to let everyone know Elvis was coming, but it was still an amazing turn out for a singer who had not appeared in concert or recorded any fresh material for nearly two years.

Are You Lonesome Tonight?

As well as appearing with Frank Sinatra, Elvis recorded some classic songs including 'Are You Lonesome Tonight?' and 'It's Now or Never' in the spring of 1960. 'It's Now or Never' went on to sell nine million copies. The LP 'Elvis is Back' was also released and stayed in the *Billboard* chart for 56 weeks. The fans soon resumed their old habits, and Elvis was almost besieged wherever he went.

GI Blues

In May 1960, Elvis began filming *GI Blues*, a musical comedy in which he played a singer serving in the Army. The story borrowed heavily from recent events in Elvis's own life – his character is not only stationed in Germany, he is also in a tank division. The film was aimed at a general market rather than teenagers and Elvis appears more mature and responsible.

Made in Hollywood

Elvis and Juliet Prowse in a scene from *GI Blues*. All the scenes featuring Elvis were shot in Hollywood, with the location footage in Germany done at a different time.

GI Blues: a tremendous success

Although longer since he left the Army, Elvis's hair was never again worn in the duck-tail style he had before. *GI Blues* was tremendously successful at the box office, ranking 14th in box office receipts. Critics approved of his new image – but Elvis worried that the musical numbers did not fit into the plot well and the songs were not as good as in some of his previous films. Despite his fears, the soundtrack album stayed in the charts longer than many of his others and soon reached No.1.

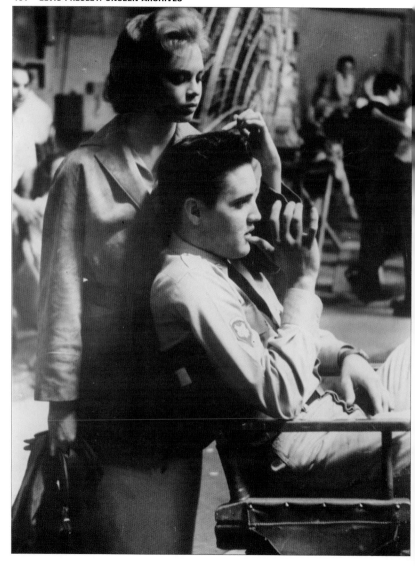

Co-starring Juliet Prowse

Juliet Prowse watches Elvis try the double bass. As well as Juliet, the film also starred Sigrid Maier, Leticia Roman, Robert Ivers and James Douglas. It was the last movie in the original three-picture contract with Hal Wallis, but the Colonel soon began to negotiate another, similar deal.

Opposite: Co-star Juliet Prowse was the girlfriend of Frank Sinatra – who was not amused when rumours of an affair with Elvis reached him.

Visited by royalty

While filming was in progress, a stream of important visitors came to see Elvis on set. In just one day he welcomed the King and Queen of Thailand, the wife and daughter of the Brazilian president, and three Scandinavian princesses (seen above) – not to mention Pat Boone, Minnie Pearl and Ernie Ford. The Colonel made sure that everyone knew that he was responsible for the royals – he was tirelessly dedicated to promoting anything that involved 'his boy'.

Opposite: A handsome and relaxed Elvis poses in his costume for *GI Blues*.

Elvis takes a gamble

Elvis with Bobby Darin who was appearing at the Hotel Saharah at Las Vegas. Elvis was in Las Vegas on a short holiday, after filming on *GI Blues* was finished. During the weekend, he lost $10,000 at the crap tables.

Opposite: When *GI Blues* was shown in Mexico City it caused a riot – and the Mexican government promptly banned all Elvis films.

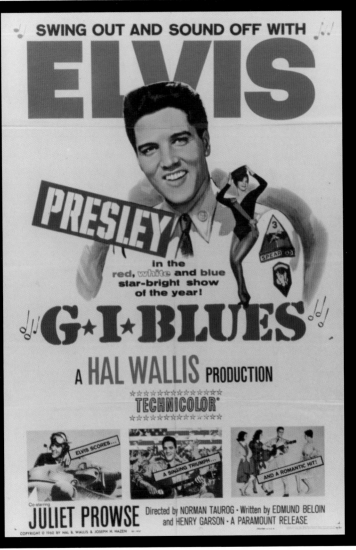

August 1960: Elvis gets serious in Flaming Star

In his next film, *Flaming Star*, Elvis plays Pacer Burton, the son of a white settler and a Kiowa Indian woman, played by Dolores Del Rio. An uprising by the Indians forces Pacer to chose sides – and the storyline also covers the prejudice he encounters as a half-caste. With a respected director, Don Siegal, and a cast of notable actors, *Flaming Star* was the serious movie that Elvis had been wanting to make for some time. Although a version with four songs was also shot, the final release only had two – which greatly disappointed the fans.

The problems with prejudice that Pacer Burton experiences in *Flaming Star* were taken by some to be a veiled reference to the problems of African-Americans during their struggle for civil rights in the 1950s and 1960s.

Native American stuntmen taught Elvis how to handle his pistol correctly. The story was based on a popular novel by Clair Huffaker but had taken some years to bring to the screen.

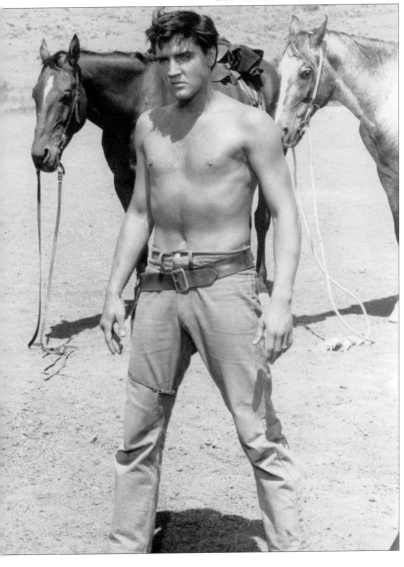

Elvis takes a break

Above: Elvis protects Dolores Del Rio as the two of them escape from pursuers. Although *Flaming Star* was a critical success, it did not do as well at the box office as many of Elvis's other films.

Left: Elvis with Barbara Eden, who played his romantic interest in *Flaming Star*. She later went on to star in the television series *I Dream of Jeannie*.

Opposite: Although Elvis made it through all the rough and tumble of filming without accident, he broke his finger while playing touch football between takes.

Christmas at Graceland 1960

Elvis pictured outside Graceland with his Rolls-Royce, just before Christmas 1960.

Opposite top: Chief Wah-Nee-Ota inducts Elvis into the Los Angeles Indian Tribal Council in recognition of his role as a half-caste in *Flaming Star*.

Opposite bottom: Elvis with the Jordanaires recording a song for the soundtrack of one of his films.

CHAPTER FOUR

Are You Lonesome Tonight?

A thoughtful Elvis strums his guitar in a still from the 1961 movie, *Wild in the Country*.

During 1961 Elvis performed live only three times – two concerts at the Ellis Auditorium in Memphis and a charity event for the USS *Arizona* at Bloch Arena at Pearl Harbor, Hawaii. The live appearances had become a danger to all concerned – he had to arrive and leave in the greatest secrecy as the fans behaved so wildly in their attempts to reach him that there was a real risk that someone would soon get hurt. Elvis was also now concentrating on his film career, and since he went on to make three pictures a year for most of the rest of the 1960s there was little time left for concert tours.

The overall quality of Elvis's films has sometimes been criticized, particularly since at the beginning of his movie career several of his directors and fellow actors thought he was capable of even better things. However, many of his pictures were not only highly successful at the box office but were also well received by the critics. In common with many other musical and comedy stars, almost all his movies were specifically written as a vehicle for their leading man – feel-good stories with lots of songs worked into the script. Elvis himself knew that he could also do darker and more complex roles, given the chance – he said several times in interviews that he wanted to become a serious actor and do dramatic parts. Some people blamed the Colonel for Elvis's failure to widen the range of roles he played, feeling that the desire to make ever more money made the Colonel short-sighted with regard to wider issues. His tireless negotiating for higher fees was certainly a factor in encouraging the studios to play safe and go for the tried and tested to protect their investment. *Flaming Star* and *Wild in the Country* had taken a different line and moved away from singing but they did less well at the box office. On the other hand, *Blue Hawaii*, a lightweight musical comedy

Tuesday Weld played an uneducated country girl with an illegitimate child in *Wild in the Country*. Throughout filming, there were rumours in the press that the two of them planned to get married. They did become close and stayed friends for many years afterwards.

built round an exotic location, was a massive hit. Several of the later films were therefore made to a similar formula, but unfortunately some of them suffered from short schedules and tight budgets. Elvis knew that they were not all that he wanted to do, that he had other ambitions to fulfil, but no one could deny that they were making money. Although he was offered some interesting and controversial roles, the Colonel turned them down, both because they did not fit the formula he had established and because they would not have been so lucrative.

Meanwhile, Elvis's personal life was as complicated as ever. At the beginning of the 1960s he was still dating Anita, but seeing other girls whenever she was not around – the Memphis Mafia were always there to cover for him. He had also remained in touch with Priscilla in Germany, and in March 1962 he began to talk to her parents about the possibility of her coming over to America. Understandably they were not sure about the idea, but he arranged for her to stay 'officially' with friends. Priscilla was still only 17, and Elvis himself was conscious of the potential problems if the press found out he was seeing such a young girl. Priscilla finally arrived in Los Angeles and after a few days they left to see Las Vegas, but all too soon she had to return. Despite all their precautions, Anita knew what was happening and decided it was time to move on.

Priscilla returned a few months later, to spend the Christmas holidays with Elvis at Graceland. Again the time seemed too short, so Elvis came up with the idea that she should stay in America and finish her schooling at a local Catholic school. Her parents refused to consider it at first, but eventually they gave in. Priscilla moved in with Dee and Vernon and was enrolled in the Immaculate Conception High School, but since Elvis was away in Hollywood working on yet another film, she soon moved into Graceland. When he was at home they did everything together and he began to mould her into his perfect woman, but she found it difficult to get used to having so many people around. In Germany only a couple of his cronies had been with him, so they had often had time alone together. Now there always seemed to be a crowd of people and she often felt out of place amongst the Memphis Mafia and their older wives and girlfriends.

Things soon became even more complicated. The co-star of Elvis's next movie was Ann-Margret, and she and Elvis quickly realized that they were kindred spirits. Unlike

Priscilla, who was shy and terrified of putting a foot wrong with Elvis's entourage, Ann-Margret was full of energy and mischief and soon came to be regarded as one of the boys. Several people commented that they had never seen Elvis so happy, and word began to leak into the papers that she and Elvis were an item. It came to a head when Ann-Margret went to London for the royal première of her previous film and the British press reported that she had talked of marrying Elvis. The US papers quickly picked up the story; Priscilla was furious and upset – and so was Elvis. He assured the press that if he planned to marry they would hear about it from him, and to Priscilla he denied everything and told her she was the only woman for him. Ann-Margret later refuted the claims that she had said anything but, although she and Elvis remained in contact and continued to see each other in secret, from then on they began to drift apart.

By 1964 The Beatles had hit America and were blasting through the charts, but Elvis had not had a major hit since 'Return to Sender' in 1962. He had somehow lost his direction and he felt increasingly unhappy, lonely and empty. At this point he met hairdresser Larry Geller, who introduced him to spirituality and the search for self-knowledge. Most of those around him did not share his interest and resented the newcomer, but Elvis became immersed in his new way of life and spent as much time as possible studying over the next couple of years. Despite this, he was also still relying heavily on amphetamines – as were most members of the Memphis Mafia. It all came to a head when he missed the start of filming on his new picture, *Clambake*, saying he was sick. The Colonel demanded a doctor's certificate and although a local doctor, Dr George Nichopoulos, provided one, the Colonel decided things had gone far enough. Elvis was not focusing on business – and since the movies were currently not making as much money as they had, this was no time for 'his boy' to become unreliable. The Colonel fired some of the entourage and made sure Geller was gradually excluded, after which Elvis soon began to return to his old interests.

There was now also Elvis's forthcoming wedding to prepare for. Priscilla had been living at Graceland for more than three years and both she and her father – and the Colonel – had been dropping heavy hints to Elvis about fulfilling his commitments. They finally became engaged at Christmas 1966, and the wedding was set for 1 May 1967, in

Las Vegas. The ceremony itself was private – even the Memphis Mafia and their wives and girlfriends were excluded, although they were invited to the reception. Afterwards the newlyweds went back to Palm Springs and then on to the Flying Circle G in Mississippi, the ranch that Elvis had bought earlier that year. Although several members of the entourage came with them, Priscilla later said it was an idyllic time in which their privacy was respected and she was able to enjoy looking after her new husband herself. At the end of the month they returned to Graceland and had another big reception for those who had missed the first. Within a few weeks, Priscilla realized she was pregnant. At first she was upset, because for the first time she had been feeling a real part of Elvis's life in America and now everything would inevitably change, but Elvis was delighted at the prospect of becoming a father. After Lisa Marie Presley was born on 1 February 1968, Elvis announced that he was the happiest man in the world.

Although his personal life seemed to have settled down, the problems in Elvis's career now came to a head. The fans were less devoted to seeing Elvis in every movie he made, and although a gospel album, 'How Great Thou Art', was selling steadily, his other records were not doing that well. The songs being supplied for film soundtracks were often so formulaic that even the Colonel was moved to protest. Unfortunately, much of the reason for that went back to the old arrangements he himself had set up for writers requiring them to forgo part of their royalty before Elvis would record their song. Understandably, the best material was now no longer offered to him.

A change of direction was clearly needed and Elvis was ready to make it. The Colonel had arranged for him to appear in a TV special, which was to be broadcast just before Christmas 1968. It was to be recorded before a live audience – the first time Elvis had sung on stage for seven years. The Colonel wanted 'his boy' to sing a straightforward selection of Christmas songs, but NBC producer Bob Finkel convinced Elvis to go for a radical change of image. Director Steve Binder put together a show that featured Elvis in black leather belting out his rock 'n' roll hits, and finished with a brand new song, 'If I Can Dream'. It was a total triumph. Everyone had forgotten what Elvis was capable of and hearing him sing the old hits with an exciting new freshness was a revelation to many.

Elvis himself was now determined to return to touring. From his new position of

strength, the Colonel arranged a four-week booking at the brand-new International Hotel that was due to open in Las Vegas that July. It was certainly a gamble: Elvis's only previous appearance in Las Vegas had been a disaster; the room he was being expected to fill had a capacity almost twice those that current major headliners played; and it would all take place in a full glare of publicity. Meanwhile, some changes had also been made in terms of how the records were recorded. The last few studio sessions in Nashville had been fairly disastrous, with only the minimum usable material laid down. Elvis was persuaded to try American, a small new studio in Memphis that had produced a string of hits under the direction of its principal owner, Chips Moman. The sessions were an unqualified success and Elvis recorded some of his best material to date, with the first single released, 'In the Ghetto', giving him a major hit and another gold record.

The opening night in Las Vegas on 31 July 1969, was the first time Elvis had performed a full concert in public for more than eight years. He was visibly nervous beforehand, but when he came out on stage and launched into his first number, his uninhibited love for the music combined with his instinctive sense of what the audience wanted created a sensational show. Those watching exploded with excitement and even the critics spoke of a mesmerizing performance. By the end of the run his female fans were throwing underwear onto the stage, just like in the old days. The hotel management were quick to pick up their option on further shows, booking Elvis to appear twice a year for the next five years.

Unfortunately, while Elvis was now riding high in his career, his personal life was not going so well; although outwardly they appeared the perfect couple, Elvis and Priscilla were already having problems. After Lisa Marie was born, Elvis had made it plain to Priscilla that he was no longer physically attracted to her. Unhappy and unfulfilled, Priscilla had begun an affair with her dance instructor. No one dared tell Elvis – but it was only a matter of time before the marriage would begin to fall apart.

Opposite: Elvis with Hope Lange in *Wild in the Country*. Although there were originally no songs in the movie, several were added after it was noted that the previous serious film, *Flaming Star*, was not doing as well at the box office.

Fans cluster around a lei-clad Elvis as he stands in Los Angeles airport before flying to Hawaii to star in his next movie, *Blue Hawaii*. He was also scheduled to make several benefit appearances during his three-week stay on the island.

Can't Help Falling in Love

During a scene from *Blue Hawaii*, Elvis sings to a bevy of Hawaiian beauties. A musical comedy, this was one of the most commercially successful of Elvis's films. 'Can't Help Falling in Love', from the soundtrack of *Blue Hawaii*, was released as a single in October 1961 and went on to become a massive hit that year.

Behind bars again!

In *Blue Hawaii*, Elvis played Chad Gates, the son of a wealthy plantation owner. Pressured by his parents to give up his easy-going lifestyle to help run the family business, Chad disappears to the beach to play music with his native Hawaiian friends.

Opposite top: In a scene from the film, Guy Lee as Ping Pong tries to spray water at Roland Winters as Fred Gates, Elvis, Angela Lansbury as Sarah Lee Gates and John Archer as Fred Kelman.

Opposite bottom: The soundtrack of *Blue Hawaii* featured 14 other numbers as well as 'Can't Help Falling in Love'. The music ranged across several musical styles. There were extensive shots of the Hawaiian scenery, with shooting at Waikiki Beach, Hanauma Bay and Ala Moana Park.

Dreading deep water...

Opposite: Angela Lansbury was cast as Elvis's mother – although she was only 35 at the time.

Left: Joan Blackman with Elvis on the beach. During the filming of *Blue Hawaii*, Elvis revealed that he was apprehensive in deep water. Director Norman Taurog gave him the option of doing scenes on the beach instead, but Elvis bravely faced his fear and most of them were shot in or on the ocean, as originally called for in the script.

Follow That Dream!

Right: Elvis and co-star Joanne Moore enjoy a little dalliance on the beach, in a scene from *Follow That Dream.* The title song from the movie was released in April 1962 and went on to become a big hit.

Above: Elvis got lost on his way to the wedding of his secretary, Pat Boyd, to one of the Memphis Mafia, Bobby West, and so he missed the ceremony. He arrived just in time for the reception.

Opposite: Blue Hawaii was released not long before Christmas 1961, and quickly turned a profit. It grossed almost $5 million and the soundtrack album became the fastest-selling LP of that year.

Battered and bruised

In *Kid Galahad*, Elvis played a gallant boxer – although the bruises are the work of the studio make-up department. He was unhappy about his appearance because his weight had recently shot up, and he did not enjoy making the movie. One bright spot was taking boxing lessons from former welterweight champion Mushy Callahan, for whom Elvis felt deep respect. He tried to impress co-star Charles Bronson, who was playing his trainer in the film, but the veteran actor had little time for him.

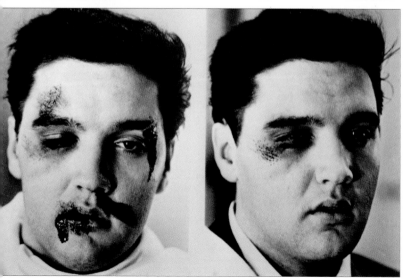

1962: Return to Sender

Above: In a fit of anger, Elvis slugs Jeremy Slate, who has tried to steal his girl. *Girls! Girls! Girls!* was shot in Hawaii.

Right: Laurel Goodwin had the part of Elvis's love interest in *Girls! Girls! Girls!*

Elvis poses for stills during the filming of *Girls! Girls! Girls!*. Many well-respected musical and comedy stars have appeared in movies tailored specifically round their talents – and Elvis was not the only popular music star to do so. Frankie Avalon, Herman's Hermits and The Beatles all made such pictures, which were marketed mainly to young audiences.

Summer of 1962

Elvis and his entourage arrive in Seattle, accompanied by police officers. They had come to the city for location filming for *It Happened at the World's Fair* – the 1962 World's Fair was being held there at the time.

Opposite: Elvis gets a manicure on Seattle's monorail. He and the guys were prone to elaborate jokes to liven up the boredom of filming. One of their favourites was to call for room service after having removed all the furniture from the room – then to have it all back in place by the time the manager arrived.

$9300 wardrobe

The storyline of *Fun in Acapulco* had Elvis as a former trapeze artist, who develops a phobia after his partner is severely injured. He gets a job as a lifeguard in a luxurious Mexican resort instead, and falls in love with the hotel's social director, played by Ursula Andress. Exteriors were shot on location in Mexico, but Elvis stayed on the Paramount lot in Hollywood. *Fun in Acapulco* went on to become the top-grossing movie of 1963.

Opposite: Hitching a ride to the World's Fair. The Colonel always made sure there were plenty of photographers on set, and planted a story about Elvis's new wardrobe that had been supplied for the film. Hollywood couturier Sy Devore explained that the entire wardrobe cost $9300 – but did not include underwear as Elvis did not wear any.

1963: Viva Las Vegas

Ann-Margret and Elvis during filming of *Viva Las Vegas* for MGM in 1963. Ann-Margret was known as the 'female Elvis Presley' because of her sensual performing style, and rumours quickly began circulating that the two stars were having an affair. This time the rumours were true – despite the fact that Priscilla was already quietly living at Graceland.

On-screen chemistry...

Elvis and Ann-Margret study one of the songs that they are to sing in *Viva Las Vegas*. Because of the sexual chemistry between the two stars, the musical numbers in the film vibrate with a sensual passion not found in Elvis's other movies.

Opposite: Elvis and Ann-Margret shared a love of motorcycles – much to the consternation of production staff, since an accident to either of them could have delayed filming for many weeks.

Elvis and Ann-Margret get serious

The affair with Ann-Margret was the most serious that Elvis had with any of his co-stars. However, she was serious about her career and certainly did not want to give it up for marriage at this stage. Elvis also had Priscilla to consider – to get her father's permission to bring her over to the US from Germany, he had apparently promised that they would get married one day.

Just good friends?

Even after their romance cooled, Elvis and Ann-Margret stayed close friends – right up to the end of his life – and he always sent flowers to her on opening nights.

Priscilla stays out of the public eye

Elvis enjoys a few nights off in Las Vegas. Priscilla was never seen with him in public during this period – everyone was afraid of what the press would make of the fact that he had such a young girl staying in his home, even though she was well-chaperoned.

Meeting Jim Brown

Above: A group of Las Vegas showgirls are eager to chat to their celebrity guest.

Opposite: During a break in filming of their respective movies, Jim Brown drops in on Elvis for a chat. Elvis had long been an admirer of the other actor's work and had wanted to meet him for some time. Elvis was currently filming *Roustabout*, in which he played a carnival hand with a knack for getting into trouble. Barbara Stanwyck was the boss and the two stars initially did not get on. Later they became friends and Elvis said the experience of working with her had inspired him to become a better actor.

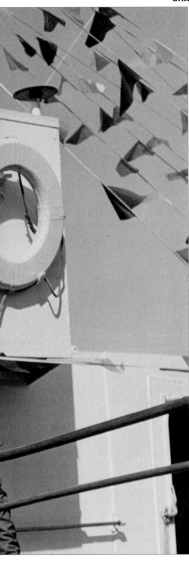

White elephant…

In 1964, it was announced that Elvis had bought the USS *Potomac* for $55,000. The boat had been President Roosevelt's 'floating White House' during the Second World War but had been pensioned off from active service to act as a tourist attraction in Long Beach. The owners had planned to auction it on the 82nd anniversary of Roosevelt's birth and the Colonel decided that Elvis should buy it and present it to the March of Dimes. Unfortunately it was far too expensive to maintain for the March of Dimes to accept, so they turned down the offer.

The Coast Guard Unit in Miami also refused to accept it and newspapers began to refer to the *Potomac* as a 'white elephant'. Finally, the St Jude Hospital in Memphis, a research centre that investigated serious childhood diseases, decided they would take it. The boat was hurriedly painted to impress the press – but there had only been time to do one side. The charity had been founded by comedian Danny Thomas, and he officially accepted the *Potomac* from Elvis in a dedication ceremony held at Long Beach in February. In the background, the Colonel smokes one of his trademark cigars.

March 1964:
Filming begins on Roustabout

Barbara Stanwyck and Elvis enjoy a ride on the carousel. *Roustabout* was set against the background of a small American carnival – a life that the Colonel certainly knew inside out. He had suggested the original idea back in 1961, and as the script developed he came up with many pieces of 'carny' business to include in the story.

Elvis does his own stunts

Part of the action for *Roustabout* was filmed on location, at Thousand Oaks just northwest of Los Angeles and at the Hidden Valley Ranch in California. Elvis insisted on doing a fight sequence himself, and was hit on the head. He needed four stitches but, since the script called for him to be ridden off the road on his motorcycle, the genuine injury was used and filming continued.

The Colonel's offer

In the story, the carnival boss discovers Elvis's singing talent and uses him to attract crowds to the show.

Opposite top: As well as Barbara Stanwyck, the movie also co-stared Joan Freeman as the girl who fights Elvis all the way, but who eventually falls in love with him. The Stanwyck part was originally offered to Mae West, but she turned it down.

Opposite bottom: *Tickle Me* was Elvis's first picture for Allied Artists. His salary of $750,000 was half the budget, and he also had a 50% share of the profits. Allied Artists was in financial trouble and the Colonel offered to let them out of their agreement, but studio head Steve Broidy refused.

Taking on the bad guys

Director Norman Taurog, on his fifth Presley film, was asked to try to bring *Tickle Me* in under budget – both to help Allied Artists and to ensure the picture was completed. Since he was a fast and efficient worker, who got on well with Elvis, he managed to come in under what was already a tight costing.

Above: Enjoying a joke with one of his co-stars on the set of *Tickle Me*. Away from the cameras, Elvis had found a much more serious interest. He had recently met Larry Geller, a hairdresser who had introduced him to alternative religion.

Opposite: Elvis tackles the bad guy. *Tickle Me* saved Allied Artists from going under, its gross only coming in behind that of *55 Days in Peking* and *El Cid* in the company's history. It also made the usual profit for Elvis and the Colonel.

Tickle Me!

In *Tickle Me*, Elvis played an unemployed rodeo star, who accepts a job at a health farm. He helps one of the girls escape from the clutches of villains, who are looking for treasure. The health farm setting ensured that there was plenty of opportunity to feature scantily-clad starlets.

Cutting costs...

One way in which the Colonel maximized profits from *Tickle Me* was to arrange with Allied that the film soundtrack would only utilize songs already recorded by Elvis – which he guaranteed would not have appeared on a single or EP. In this way they could avoid the costs of recording original soundtrack material, while at the same time still being able to release a soundtrack record.

Many of the songs featured in Elvis's movies are very good – there is 'Return to Sender' from *Girls! Girls! Girls!*, 'Wolf Call' from *Girl Happy* and 'Can't Help Falling in Love' from *Blue Hawaii*. However, since *Tickle Me* did not have an original score, it had to rely on the quality of the songs that the Colonel picked out – although Elvis made the final selection.

1965: Come into the desert…

Opposite: Harum Scarum was a light-hearted film, set in the desert, produced by Sam Katzman and directed by Gene Nelson. The costumes were deliberately designed to make Elvis look like a modern Rudolf Valentino.

Above: While Elvis was making *Frankie and Johnnie* for United Artists, he was deeply absorbed by studies of religion, philosophy and the occult. Co-star Donna Douglas was both religious and spiritual, and Elvis spent hours with her discussing the books they had each read. He was rather overweight during filming, but his costumes were cleverly cut to hide it.

Paradise regained in 1965

In *Paradise, Hawaiian Style*, Elvis played Rick Richards, a helicopter pilot who operates a charter service. He had always enjoyed being in Hawaii before, but this time reporters noted that he seemed rather depressed. Nevertheless, he threw himself into the making of the film, in which he sang some traditional Hawaiian folk songs.

Elvis had not had a song in the charts for a while, but now 'Crying in the Chapel', which had been recorded some time before and released in April 1965, was a top ten hit.

Action hero

The typical Presley hero was always a man of action, often with an interesting or unusual job – who could also sing. In *Spinout*, a film for MGM again directed by Norman Taurog, he was a racing driver. The 1929 Duesenberg in which he is supposed to enter the Santa Fe Road Race was a priceless classic car. Despite its glamorous settings and glimpses of a wealthy lifestyle, the movie did not do well at the box office. However, his new single, 'Love Letters', was released in June 1966 and soon went into the top 20.

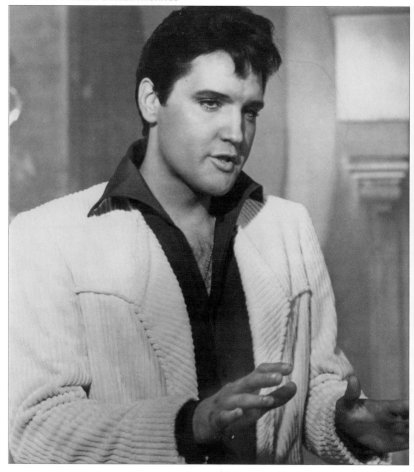

Disco time…

The producers of Elvis's films always kept an eye on what was going on in popular culture. When European discotheques were all the rage, Elvis appeared in *Double Trouble*, which was set in the discotheques of London and Amsterdam. Elvis did not go on location abroad to film – all his scenes were shot in Hollywood. During the course of the eight-week shooting schedule, Elvis presented his leading lady, Annette Day, with a blue and white Mustang.

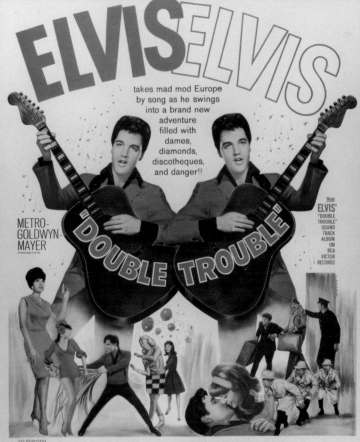

Elvis in a scene from *Clambake*. He was now filming for much of the year – *Easy Come, Easy Go* had begun shooting just three weeks after *Double Trouble* had finished, although there was then a three-month break before *Clambake* began. The review of *Easy Come, Easy Go* in *Variety* said, 'Anyone who has seen similar movies recognizes the superior quality of Presley's movies: the story makes sense; the songs are better, and better motivated; cast and direction are stronger; production values are first-rate.'
Opposite: Double Trouble was released in April 1967 and – although it did steady business – it did not make the kind of profits that Presley pictures were expected to bring in.

1967: Priscilla and Elvis say 'I do'

On 1 May 1967, Elvis and Priscilla Beaulieu are married by Nevada Supreme Court Justice David Zenoff, in a private ceremony held in a suite in the English-Tudor-style Aladdin Hotel in Las Vegas.

'It was about time' says Elvis

After the eight-minute ceremony was over, a press conference was held in the Aladdin Room of the hotel. Priscilla showed off her three-carat diamond ring and the happy couple kissed for the benefit of photographers. Reporters asked Elvis why he had finally decided to get married, and he replied, 'Well, I guess it was about time.' Priscilla's father told the newsmen that he had known from the beginning that the two of them would get married one day. Priscilla said later that they had both been so nervous before the ceremony that neither of them had slept the previous night.

Celebrating in style

There were over one hundred people at the reception, eating a buffet banquet while a string trio played romantic ballads – including some of the groom's hits. However, most members of the Memphis Mafia had been excluded from the actual ceremony – lack of space in the suite was cited as the reason – and were invited to the reception only. It caused some resentment, and marked the beginning of disaffection in the Mafia ranks.

Man and wife

The happy couple returned to
Palm Springs after the reception,
but three days later left for
Memphis and on to the Circle G
Ranch. Although most of the
Memphis Mafia came with them,
living on the ranch without the
household staff gave Priscilla a
chance to 'play house' and look
after her new husband herself. At
the end of the month, they held
another wedding ceremony at
Graceland – a less formal affair
that included the entire Graceland
staff and all Elvis's uncles, aunts
and cousins, as well as his doctor,
dentist, painter, horse trainer and
electrician.

Love interest

Elvis's co-star and love-interest on *Speedway* was Nancy Sinatra (opposite), and rumours circulated in the press that the two of them were having an affair in real life. They had been linked romantically several times previously but Elvis just liked to flirt with any available woman.

Nancy and Elvis

Despite all the rumours, after Lisa Marie was born it was Nancy Sinatra who held a baby shower for Priscilla.

Opposite: When asked by a journalist what kind of part he played in *Speedway*, Elvis answered, 'I'm kinduva singin' millionaire-playboy-race driver, sir.' The journalist went on to ask if Elvis had ever played such a part before, and he replied, 'Only about 25 times, sir.'

Off to the movies again…

In *Speedway*, Elvis played a racing driver for the third time and it was director Norman Taurog's eighth Presley picture. Many of the Memphis Mafia had small roles in the movie – and even Taurog's, small granddaughter had a part.

And baby makes three

On 1 February 1968, Priscilla gave birth to a baby girl. Hundreds of fans, nurses, patients and members of the press were waiting to see the new family leave the hospital and drive off in a fleet of Cadillacs and Lincolns.

Welcome Lisa Marie

Priscilla left the Baptist Memorial Hospital in Memphis four days after the birth of Lisa Marie, escorted by Elvis, Vernon and a host of others.

Proud parents

After the birth of his daughter, Elvis told everyone that he was the happiest man in the world. He had often told people over the years that if he had a daughter he would name her Gladys after his mother, but they had finally selected the name Lisa Marie. Both denied there was any significance in either name – although the Colonel's wife was called Marie.

Fun on location in 1967

In *Stay Away, Joe*, Elvis's character was an Indian rodeo rider, Joe Whitecloud, and the storyline pitted Indian ingenuity against government bureaucracy. There were originally only three songs – another was added later.

Opposite top: On the set, Elvis appeared warm and relaxed.

Opposite bottom: *Stay Away, Joe* had a good cast, with veteran actors Burgess Meredith, Thomas Gomez and Katy Jurado. They all had fun on location – even the Colonel joined in, making a promotional calendar out of a picture of himself taken by the pool with a snarling face and several days' growth of beard.

Charity concert

In June 1968, Elvis and Priscilla flew to Honolulu to visit the USS *Arizona* memorial, the fund raising for which Elvis had boosted with a charity concert.

Opposite: A publicity photograph of a more mature Elvis, taken in 1968.

Elvis's change of image

As well as Elvis and Priscilla, the party travelling to Honolulu included several members of the Memphis Mafia and their wives. They were also planning to attend a karate championship at the Honolulu International Centre, which was staged by Ed Parker, an old friend of Elvis. On his return from the holiday, Elvis was thinner than he had been for several years and had grown his sideburns longer.

1968:
Live a Little,
Love a Little

Elvis in *Live a Little, Love a Little*, a comedy film that was based on a popular novel by Dan Greenburg, *Kiss My Firm but Pliant Lips*. Again the director was Norman Taurog and the screenplay included only four songs.

Elvis tires of movie-making

In *Live a Little, Love a Little*, Elvis played a successful photographer. By this time he had decided that he wanted to stop making movies but, because of the Colonel's habit of negotiating block contracts, he was contractually obliged to make several more.

Backstage with the 'Welsh Elvis'

A publicity shot from *Live a Little, Love a Little*, with a relaxed and casual Elvis.

Opposite top: Live a Little, Love a Little was released in October 1968, but neither the single nor the film did very well. It seemed as if Elvis's career had stalled, and something bold was needed to get it going again.

Opposite bottom: Elvis and Priscilla visit Tom Jones backstage at his show in the Flamingo Hotel in Las Vegas. Tom Jones was often compared to an early Elvis in style – and in his appeal to the female fans.

Comeback king

A publicity shot for the forthcoming *Comeback Special* gives little idea of the new-look Elvis that is about to burst onto the TV screen.

Opposite: In his last few films Elvis made a break from the kind of things he had done before. *Charro!* was a hard-hitting western, in which the fans were treated to a bearded and rugged Elvis.

Reformed outlaw

Elvis's character in *Charro!* is a former outlaw, who comes over to the side of law enforcement and then has to stand up to the members of his former gang – who try to frame him for the theft of a valuable cannon that belongs to the Mexican government. Elvis looks unkempt in a dusty outfit and is almost unrecognizable.

The Trouble with Girls in 1968

Above: The Trouble With Girls was set in the 1920s, with Elvis as the manager of a chautauqua – a travelling college that brought culture to rural areas and isolated villages.

Below: Elvis doesn't appear until about one-third of the way into the movie. His main role is to hold together the various sub-plots.

Christmas 1968: Back to his roots

A leather-clad Elvis shows how it used to be, in the *Comeback Special* aired on NBC at Christmas. The Colonel had originally wanted him merely to sing a few Christmas songs, but NBC producer Steve Binder persuaded him to go back to his roots. He challenged Elvis to walk down the street and see if he was recognized by young people. Elvis was reluctant, since he had not been out without an escort for some years, but he decided to try. When no-one recognized him, he agreed that his career needed a major boost – which meant going against the Colonel's wishes.

Hit album follows Comeback Special

The *Comeback Special* featured live segments, pre-filmed concert sequences and casual jamming sessions, and loosely told the story of a young singer finding fame. The critics were ecstatic, praising both his performance and charisma. The show was the highest-rated programme that week, and the album that followed was also a hit.

The King is back!

The leather suit that Elvis wore for the *Comeback Special* had been specially tailored for him by Bill Belew, who went on to design several of the jumpsuits that Elvis wore in later years. He looked younger and more handsome than he had done for many years.

Return to touring

After he filmed the concert sequences for the *Comeback Special*, Elvis decided that he wanted to return to touring.

If I Can Dream

Elvis wore several different outfits during the various sections of the
Comeback Special. At the end, dressed in a white suit, he sang 'If I Can Dream'
which had been specially written to close the show. It had reached
No 12 in the charts by January 1969, and went on to become yet another
millionseller.

Change of habit

Elvis chatting to Colonel Tom Parker during a break in filming on *Change of Habit*. Elvis played a doctor working in a big city slum, with Mary Tyler Moore as one of three young nuns assigned to do social work in his clinic. Since she is in plain clothes Elvis does not realize she is a nun and falls in love with her, and she must decide between him and the Church. The movie did not reveal which path she took, leaving the audience to decide for themselves.

Standing ovation for live performance

At a press conference following the opening night of the first of the Las Vegas shows in summer 1969. Newsmen from all over the world had gathered to see him perform and Elvis told them 'I'm really glad to be back in front of a live audience. I don't think I have ever been more excited than I was tonight.' The show had been the first time he had performed in public for more than eight years, and he had received four standing ovations.

'Suspicious Minds' was released the following September – it went on to become a top ten single and one of Elvis's signature tunes. In 1969, Elvis also had several other top ten hits – including 'Don't Cry Daddy' and 'In the Ghetto'.

Three today!

Priscilla, Lisa Marie and Elvis in an official photograph to mark Lisa Marie's third birthday.

Family time

Despite the appearance of being a happy family, Priscilla was already becoming dissatisfied with their marriage. As soon as Elvis began performing again, he was spending long periods of time away from home and she and Lisa Marie were left alone. The pace of the tours meant it was difficult for wives and families to travel with the group, so Elvis himself had instigated a strict no-wives rule.

Happy birthday, Lisa Marie

To make up for his long absences, Elvis showered both Lisa Marie and Priscilla with expensive presents on both birthdays and at Christmas – but also often at other times as well. He had always been incredibly generous with his money, and often bought expensive gifts for complete strangers.

CHAPTER FIVE

Return to Sender

Even at the beginning of the 1970s, it was apparent to most people that Elvis's behaviour was becoming increasingly erratic, not only in private but also onstage. What was not so well known was that this was due to the quantity and mixture of prescription drugs he was taking; they not only caused mood swings, but also increased his paranoia – especially after there were threats to kill or kidnap him during a show. Not long afterwards, he was sworn in as a special deputy so he could carry a hand-gun, and this soon led to an obsession with collecting police badges and firearms. After meeting voice-over artist Paul Frees and learning that he worked as an undercover narcotics agent – complete with an official Bureau of Narcotics and Dangerous Drugs badge – Elvis was determined to get a BNDD badge for himself. Having failed to get one from the Bureau, Elvis simply asked President Nixon for one instead, and managed to get an invitation to the White House, as well as the sought-after badge.

It had now become evident that Elvis and Priscilla were drifting apart – although the reason for her continued absence was at first explained away as due to the work she was overseeing on a house being built in Monovale. Elvis carried on much as he had always done; there were women virtually on tap when he needed the company, and often it was indeed just that – for company. Many women said later that when they spent the night with him, nothing happened except perhaps a little kissing – he just didn't want to sleep alone. However, there were also several more prolonged affairs – Elvis had always found it impossible to be faithful to one woman for long. The drugs he was taking often made him difficult to deal with and most women soon tired of a role that was always on his terms, and often seemed to be that of mother rather

The success of the *Comeback Special* convinced Elvis to go back to touring. At the Houston Astrodome in February 1970, he shows off a new, tousled hairstyle. Although Elvis told people that he would like to do more relaxed and laid-back shows, he knew the audience expected him to throw all his energy into a performance so he continued to give them what they wanted.

:han lover.

By the end of 1971, Priscilla had developed an interest in karate – and in martial arts expert Mike Stone. After taking Lisa Marie to spend Christmas at Graceland, she told Elvis that she no longer loved him, and returned to Hollywood before the New Year. Two months later she told him about Mike Stone. Elvis was furious that she preferred another man to him, even though he had never been faithful to her, and soon began to date former beauty queen Linda Thompson, who moved into Graceland later that year.

After the success of his recent Las Vegas show, Elvis had embarked on a tour of America, breaking box office records wherever he went. He also appeared regularly for long 'residency' bookings in Las Vegas and at nearby Lake Tahoe. From 1969 to 1977, he played a total of almost 1,100 concerts, despite his failing health towards the end of that time. Although, at the start, he obviously enjoyed being back on stage, towards the end he was really just going through the motions, and even the most ardent fans were often disappointed. Many people wondered why he continued with such a punishing schedule, but it was principally for the money.

Elvis had established a costly lifestyle, with large numbers of hangers-on as well as family members relying on him for a living. He was also outrageously generous – not only to people he knew well, but also to perfect strangers. He often gave away cars, expensive jewellery, and money, and even bought houses for several of his associates. And it was not only Elvis's lifestyle that had to be maintained. The Colonel had once had a reputation for never spending his own money; he and his wife lived at the William Morris Agency's expense in a house in Palm Springs and he made sure that everyone contributed to the upkeep of his staff and office space. However, once Elvis had started to appear regularly at Las Vegas, the Colonel developed a passion for gambling and regularly lost at least $1 million a year at the roulette wheel. Many of his close associates became concerned, but found themselves unable to do anything to stop what was happening. The Colonel just told everyone to leave him alone, that it was no business of theirs how he spent his own money, but it was obvious that his gambling had become an obsession that was out of control. Ironically, before they went to Vegas, the Colonel had warned some of the members of the Memphis Mafia not to get hooked on gambling and now he had fallen into the trap himself.

Despite his problems, the Colonel was not one to neglect business and he soon had another mega-deal organized. *Elvis: Aloha From Hawaii*, was a concert on a grand scale that would be broadcast around the world by satellite. Even Elvis was caught up in the excitement of the event, losing some weight for the show and picking out songs that he had not recorded before. Linda Thompson seemed good for him: her sunny personality lifted his mood and she was happy to be with him constantly, attending to his every need. It almost seemed as if Elvis might have turned a corner, as if from now on things would improve.

Unfortunately, this was just an illusion. The Colonel could not understand why Elvis was becoming so irresponsible, and they were soon no longer communicating effectively. Things came to a head in Las Vegas when Elvis made derogatory comments onstage about the management of the Hilton hotel, which now owned the former International. The Colonel was livid and they had a furious argument, with Elvis firing the Colonel just as he quit. They did not speak to each other for several weeks afterwards.

The cocktail of drugs he was taking also made Elvis so ill that he missed several shows, and later in the year at Lake Tahoe, the same thing occurred again. In an attempt to stop what was happening, a private detective was hired to find out the source of Elvis's drug supplies. Three doctors and a dentist were identified, but little further action was taken. Those around him seemed to believe that Elvis would pull through on his own, just as he had dropped other things when they ceased to interest him.

In October 1973, Elvis's divorce from Priscilla was finalized. A few days later he was admitted to the hospital, and the papers reported he had collapsed because he was so upset about the end of his marriage. The reality was that he had suffered a serious reaction to the drugs he was taking. His doctor, George Nichopoulos, brought in a team of specialists who stabilized his condition, and then began an investigation into just what had caused the problem. Finally they discovered that Elvis was getting almost daily doses of pethidine, a painkiller, and was seriously addicted. He was also regularly taking tranquilizers, cortisone and sleeping pills, as well as adopting various quick-fix diets whenever he needed to lose weight in a hurry. All this had done him considerable physical damage. After quietly undergoing a drug withdrawl programme in the hospital, Elvis was nursed back to health. His room at Graceland was searched and all drugs removed before he returned home, where he spent the next couple of months recuperating. His collapse had scared him so much that, for a while at least, he was a good patient, and Dr Nichopoulos visited him almost daily to try and moderate his diet and to supervise his medication.

When he returned to Las Vegas towards the end of January 1974, Elvis was thinner and in better shape than he had been for some years. A few weeks after the end of that Vegas season, he began touring again, and this time Dr Nichopoulos came with him. Elvis was still taking an assortment of painkillers, tranquilizers and sleeping pills, but Dr Nichopoulos had worked out a daily programme to keep things on an even keel, adding multivitamins and substituting placebos for some of the drugs when he thought Elvis didn't really need them. Although, on the surface, things had stabilized, onstage Elvis was still behaving in an eccentric way. The music had become rather mundane, he no longer sang with any discernible emotion, and he often stopped singing and addressed the audience on any subject that happened to take his fancy, including his personal life, karate and religion.

Meanwhile, sales of his new record releases were down. His last few recording sessions had generated little suitable material – perhaps due to his health problems, or maybe just because of tiredness after years of almost continuous performing. Since RCA had purchased all rights to Elvis's back catalogue from the Colonel for $5.4 million in 1973, it now began to concentrate on releasing a series of records containing his old material; sales of these far outstripped those of Elvis's current releases and were not subject to royalties.

Elvis's commitment to his new health regime did not last long. By the end of 1974 he had put on weight again and was severely depressed. He spent his 40th birthday in seclusion, and at the end of January, was rushed back into the hospital and treated again to get his use of drugs back under control. While he was there, his father Vernon had a heart attack and joined him in the same hospital. After leaving hospital, Elvis stayed at Graceland to rest and lose more weight. Again, his resolution did not last long, and within a few months, he was gaining weight and finding the drugs he wanted,

despite all attempts to stop him. During concerts he often appeared exhausted, but the fans still loved him. In August, several shows in Las Vegas had to be cancelled due to Elvis's ill health, and he was re-admitted to hospital. By now, Linda Thompson had realized that she would never be able to save Elvis from himself, and with great reluctance she began to make a life away from him.

With cancelled engagements, a restricted touring schedule and no new record releases, there wasn't much money coming in. Vernon persuaded Elvis that they needed to cut expenses and three members of the Memphis Mafia were fired – Red and Sonny West, and Dave Hebler. Soon afterwards, the three of them got together with journalist Steve Dunleavy to write a book exposing what life had been like with Elvis. He was deeply upset at what he saw as a betrayal, and also worried about what his fans would think of some of the more lurid revelations.

With his entourage cut back to almost nothing, and Linda Thompson pursuing her own career, Elvis was feeling abandoned and alone. At this point he was introduced to Ginger Alden, a 20-year-old former beauty queen. Although many believed that she never really loved Elvis, he pursued her avidly, buying her cars and expensive presents, and soon asked her to marry him. She accompanied him on several tours and her presence seemed to give him a new lease of life for a short while.

At the end of July 1977, Lisa Marie came to Graceland for a two-week visit. Elvis seemed in a good mood for most of the time, although he was slightly edgy about his next tour. On August 15, he had a couple of teeth filled and later played some racket-ball, as usual settling down to try to sleep in the early hours of the morning. Despite three doses of medication he was unable to settle, and told Ginger that he would go to the bathroom to read. She woke up early in the afternoon of the 16th to find that she was still alone in bed, and went to investigate. She found Elvis lying on the floor of his bathroom, but she was too late. The King of Rock 'n' Roll was dead.

Opposite: The idea for the famous jumpsuits apparently came from Priscilla, who suggested Elvis should wear them on stage because they would be more comfortable and allow him to move freely.

That's The Way It Is

The premiere of *Elvis: That's The Way It* Is was in November 1970. Elvis is seen playing a guitar during one of the scenes, and he is obviously not as fit, healthy and vibrantly alive as he had appeared in the *Comeback Special* just two years earlier.

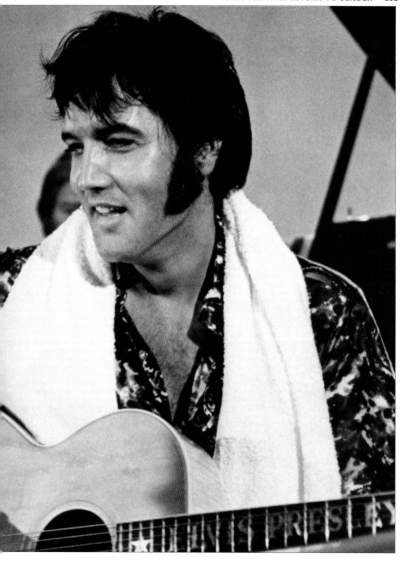

The best man

Elvis was not only best man at the marriage of his old friend George Klein – he had also generously paid for the wedding and he hugged the blushing bride for the benefit of photographers. It was held in Las Vegas on 5 December 1970, and Elvis flew a dozen of his entourage in, also paying for them to stay at the International in his suite. Klein was a former DJ and member of the Memphis Mafia, and had appeared in small parts in several of Elvis's movies.

Best of friends

Elvis, Priscilla and singer Glen Campbell. Glen Campbell had first worked as a session man for Elvis, but the two of them went on to become close friends.

Putting on a good show

Elvis and Priscilla at George Klein's wedding. Although their marriage was already in trouble, they were adept at putting on a good show in public.

Opposite bottom: The male members of the wedding party pictured together with Elvis centre stage.

Elvis and Glen

Elvis with Glen Campbell. Although he never smoked cigarettes, Elvis was very fond of cigarillos.

Opposite: One of the bridesmaids also gets a hug. The women very rarely got into the picture – although many of the Mafia were now married, their wives were very much in the background.

Meet the President...

After Elvis wrote to President Nixon, offering to help stamp out drugs, he was invited to the White House to meet the President. After Nixon agreed to give Elvis a coveted BNDD badge, Elvis stepped forward and hugged him – taking both the President and his aide off guard.

Below: Sonny West and Elvis adjust each other's ties before Sonny's wedding ceremony, which was held in Memphis.

Opposite: Nervous bridegroom Sonny West poses with Elvis. Elvis's 'fur-cloth' black bell-bottom suit had been a Christmas present from Priscilla.

Down the aisle – for the first time

Elvis, as best man, escorts Priscilla, as matron of honour, down the aisle. It was the first time they had done the walk together, as their own wedding had been a private affair in a hotel suite. *Opposite:* Sonny and his new wife, Judy, prepare to cut the cake. The reception was held in the function room of the church, but Elvis quickly got bored and invited everyone back to Graceland instead.

Law enforcers…

Back at Graceland, the men gathered for a group picture, all displaying the deputy's badges that they had recently acquired. Elvis is centre stage, flanked by Dr Nichopoulos on the left and Red West on the right, both kneeling. From left to right behind are Billy Smith, former Sheriff Bill Morris, Lamar Fike, Jerry Schilling, Sheriff Roy Nixon, Vernon Presley, Charlie Hodge, Sonny West, George Klein and Mart Lacker.

Right: Elvis proudly displays one of his guns. He had built up quite a collection and even walked down the aisle as best man wearing two guns in a shoulder holster, two pearl-handled pistols in the waistband of his pants and a derringer in his boot.

Elvis, Lisa Marie and Priscilla with Dr George Nichopoulos and his wife. Dr Nick was later accused of over-prescribing drugs to Elvis, but in fact he had fought a losing battle to stabilize an already-established heavy intake.

Star in the desert

When Elvis began
appearing in Las Vegas
regularly during the
1970s, there was no doubt
that he was a major star.
The Hilton Hotel chain
had taken over the
International in June the
previous year and before
the deal was even signed
they were anxious to make
sure that Vegas's premier
attraction would continue
to appear in their hotel.

Elvis on tour

Opposite: A shot from *That's The Way It Is*. Those involved in making the new documentary were deeply involved in their subject. They approached Elvis in concert as if he were a folk hero on a mythic journey. In addition, they had the latest mobile cameras and equipment, which brought movement and spontaneity to the filming.

As well as shots of Elvis performing, the filmmakers – Bob Abel and Pierre Adidge – included backstage material, shots of past glories and candid moments. The final movie is one of the classic records of Elvis's career.

At the beginning, Abel had told Elvis, 'I want to shoot the real you… but you've got to be open with me. If I feel that you're posing or doing something, I'll just turn the camera off.' Elvis appreciated his honesty, and from then on was committed to the project.

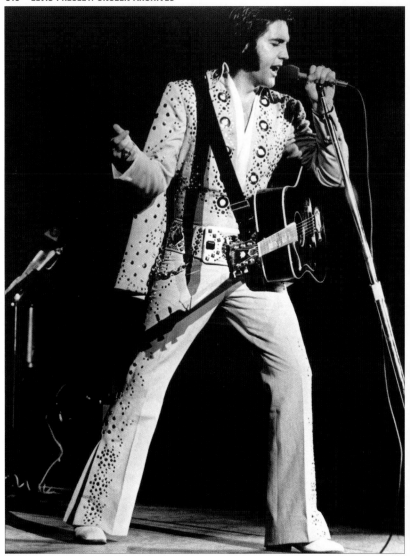

First time at Madison Square Garden

Opposite: Even the Colonel was won over by Adel and Adidge, telling them to 'Go out there and make the best Elvis movie ever.' And that's more or less what they did.

Above: At a press conference in New York, where he was appearing for the first time at Madison Square Garden, Elvis soon won over the jaded newsmen. When asked how he thought he had managed to outlast every other performer from his generation, he quickly quipped, 'I take vitamin E.'

Hard to live up to the image

At the press conference, Elvis was accompanied by both the Colonel and his father. A reporter asked Elvis if he was happy with his image, but Elvis pointed out that the image was one thing, but a human being was another. He then added, 'It's very hard to live up to an image.'

Putting on the style in Vegas

The jumpsuits that Elvis wore in Las Vegas have become a symbol that represent this stage of his career. Most of them were designed by tailor Bill Belew, and they became increasingly elaborate. Sometimes they incorporated a cape – either waist or floor-length – and they were decorated with real gemstones and semi-precious jewels.

The symbols used on some of the later costumes were of special significance to Elvis – eagles, karate symbols, tigers, peacocks, and the fans often gave these outfits special names.

World tour planned

At a press conference in Las Vegas in 1972, Elvis announced that he would soon be going on a worldwide concert tour. The idea had often been discussed before, but nothing had ever come of it – and nothing came of it this time either. Many suspected that the Colonel put a stop to Elvis touring abroad, because he himself did not have a US passport. He would therefore not be able to go and exercise control over how things were done.

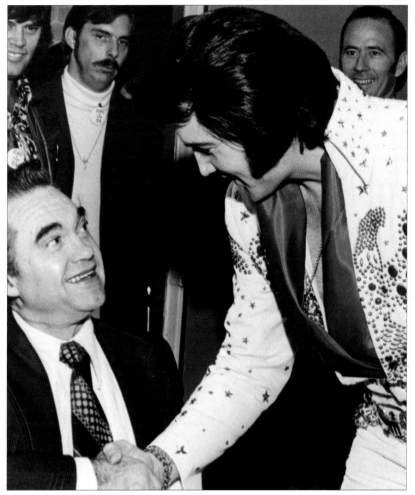

The king plays Alabama

Elvis greets Governor George C. Wallace in Montgomery, Alabama, when he performed there at the Garrett Coliseum. Governor Wallace and his family were among the audience of more than 11,000 who came to see the show.

Elvis increasingly had a problem controlling his weight. His poor diet certainly didn't help, but the additional weight was also due to lack of exercise. He was taking a dangerous combination of prescription drugs and he was hospitalized several times. Many of those close to him tried to cut his drug intake, but Elvis was used to getting his own way. Despite his bloated appearance in some of the shows, the fans still loved him and flocked to all his performances.

Last appearance

Elvis's last appearance on stage, on 26 June 1977, in Indianapolis. He had missed several shows over the previous few months, amid increasing concerns over his health. After the show he returned home the Graceland to rest and recuperate over the summer, before the start of the next tour. The next tour never happened – in fewer than two months he was dead.

The King is dead, long live the King

Above: Ginger Alden, the girlfriend who found Elvis's body, leaving the courtroom with her mother, Jo. She had been appearing before the Shelby County grand jury, who were investigating the prescription practices of Dr George Nichopoulos. *Left:* Dr George Nichopoulos had his licence to practise suspended for three months while the investigation was going on, but was eventually cleared of all charges. *Opposite:* Elvis's last appearance on stage, on 26 June 1977, in Indianapolis.

CHAPTER SIX

Only Believe

Elvis's funeral cortège was led by a silver Cadillac and a police motorcycle escort, followed by a white hearse and seventeen white limousines.

Right from the beginning, confusion surrounded the cause of Elvis's death, since the Shelby County medical examiner announced to the press that it was due to heart problems (cardiac arrhythmia, or irregular heartbeat) before the autopsy had been completed. In fact, the lab results later confirmed that his death was due to polypharmacy: traces of 14 different medications were found in Elvis's system, with codeine at ten times the recommended level. Elvis had apparently taken the drug after the dental work carried out the day before his death – despite having a mild but long-standing allergy to it. No official announcement was made about the lab results, although rumours of drug abuse quickly began to circulate in the media. In 1979, Dr Nichopoulos was charged with over-prescribing drugs to Elvis and briefly lost his medical licence, but was later found not guilty of any criminal intent.

Elvis's funeral was a private service held at Graceland, with only 200 invited guests, although thousands of fans gathered outside. A cortège of 49 cars followed the white hearse that carried his body to Forest Hill Cemetery, where he was buried next to his mother. The following day an estimated 50,000 fans visited his tomb, and Vernon requested that each should be given a flower from the wreaths and arrangements that were banked up around the cemetery. It had taken 100 vans nearly four hours to move all the floral tributes from Graceland the day before, yet within a few hours they were all gone.

Just 11 days after the burial, three men made what was thought to be a bungled attempt to steal Elvis's body. Charges were dropped after the court was convinced that they had merely been trying to prove that the coffin was empty and that Elvis was still alive. There were fears that it might happen again, so just a couple of months later, both Elvis and his mother were removed from Forest Hill Cemetery and re-interred in the Meditation Garden at Graceland. The Meditation Garden also held a memorial plaque for Elvis's stillborn twin brother, Jesse Garon Presley, and Vernon was buried there after his death in 1979.

The entire Presley estate had been left to Lisa Marie in trust until she was 25, but Priscilla and the other trustees were alarmed to discover how little money was left. After Elvis's death, the Colonel had wasted no time in arranging a new marketing deal with Vernon, which meant that for the next few years, he was earning far more from Elvis's name than the estate was. After Vernon's death in 1979, the executors of the Presley estate started an investigation and the courts later ruled that the contract Vernon had signed was void, so the Colonel had to give up all marketing rights.

In 1982, Graceland was opened to the public to raise money for Lisa Marie's inheritance, and the Presley estate also began to receive all the income generated through the use of Elvis's name. According to an estimate in *Life* magazine in 1984, the 'Elvis industry' earned ten times more in the seven years following his death than Elvis had earned in his 23 years of performing. When Lisa Marie became 25 in 1993, the estate was worth an estimated $100 million and she elected not to take over, but to leave the existing management in place. Elvis Presley Enterprises, Inc., is now run as a business, controlling the rights to Elvis's name, and Graceland is a major tourist attraction, one of the most visited historic homes in America.

Elvis is perhaps even more famous today than when he was alive. In the weeks after his funeral, radio stations around the world started to play his music again and several of his records re-entered the charts. Although his music had changed almost out of recognition in the last few years of his life, his death focused attention on the early songs, when he had been a true artist and a major influence on the development of modern music. He was posthumously inducted into the Rock and Roll, Country, and Gospel Halls of Fame – the first artist to make it into all three.

Over the years there has been a constant stream of Elvis documentaries, films and TV series, either telling his life story, looking at the making of a particular record, or discussing his death. Many people who were close to Elvis have been persuaded to write about their memories of him, and countless books and articles have been published over the years, some flattering, some condemning. In 1988, rumours spread that he had faked his own death, after a book claiming he was still alive was published, along with a tape of him apparently talking about events that had happened after 1977. The tape was later discredited, but the rumours escalated and sightings of Elvis were reported all over the place. The stories became increasingly bizarre, placing him in unlikely locations around the world, and even on the moon. A few of the more obsessive fans seized on his connection with the BNDD and insisted that he had actually gone undercover as a narcotics investigator, or that he had merely become tired of his public lifestyle and had vanished to find a quieter life elsewhere.

However, most fans are content to remember their hero by visiting places of importance to him and collecting memorabilia. In 1992, the US Postal Service was persuaded to issue an Elvis stamp. Two designs were produced – one showing Elvis as a young rocker and the other the more mature, Vegas-style Elvis. Fans were asked to vote on which one they preferred. The young rocker won hands down, and 500 million stamps were printed – more than any other similar stamp.

Every year there is a Tribute Week in Memphis around the anniversary of Elvis's death, with dozens of Elvis-related events. People flock from across the globe to take part. At regular conventions around the world, thousands of fans still gather to listen to speeches, talk about Elvis and buy Elvis products. And then there are the Elvis impersonators; although they also existed before his death, there are now thousands of them around the world, some full-time, some part-time – including several black and Asian people, women and children. Most seem to choose to portray the 1970s Las Vegas Elvis, perhaps because that look is so instantly recognizable, and they often take their role extremely seriously, buying exact replicas of his outfits and closely copying his movements and style of delivery. A few have even had plastic surgery to make them look as much like the real Elvis as possible. And some, as well as performing as Elvis, keep up the act in their everyday lives.

There can be few entertainers in the history of the world who have inspired such devotion. Years after his death, shops are still full of his records, and his image is instantly recognizable in almost every country of the world. He has become much more than just a singer who died – he is now a true American folk hero.

Elvis himself once said, 'When I was a boy, I was the hero in comic books and movies. I grew up believing in a dream. Now, I've lived it out. That's all a man can ask for.'

Elvis has left the building…

Elvis's flower-covered casket is carried into the mausoleum at Forest Hill Cemetery. The pall-bearers included Memphis Mafia members Joe Esposito, Charlie Hodge and Lamar Fike, Dr Nichopoulos, and Elvis's cousin Billy Smith.

Opposite top: The hearse with its copper casket leaves Graceland, past saluting policemen. The funeral service had been held in the living room, with a sermon by Reverend Bradley of the Wooddale Church of Christ.

Opposite bottom: Local florists were flooded with over 3,000 orders for flowers and they covered the lawn in front of Graceland. It took four hours to move the flowers to the cemetery before the funeral.

Finally at rest

After an apparent attempt was made to steal Elvis's body just after the funeral, he and his mother were both moved from Forest Hill and reburied in the Meditation Garden at Graceland, in October 1977.

Opposite top: The gray stone mausoleum was surrounded by a bank of flowers and was just a few hundred feet away from Gladys Presley's grave in the same cemetery.

One year on...

Thousands of fans poured into Memphis, bringing floral tributes to Elvis's grave at Graceland on the first anniversary of his death in 1978.

A nine-foot statue of Elvis sculpted by Eric Parks was erected on Beale Street in Memphis in 1980 – a fitting tribute to the city's famous son.

Gone, but not forgotten

Even now, fans still come to Graceland on the anniversary of Elvis's death to pay their respects and leave floral tributes to their idol. On the evening of 15 August, there is a candlelight procession at Graceland, which often takes many hours to file past his grave. It is the culmination of the Tribute Week that is held in Memphis every year.

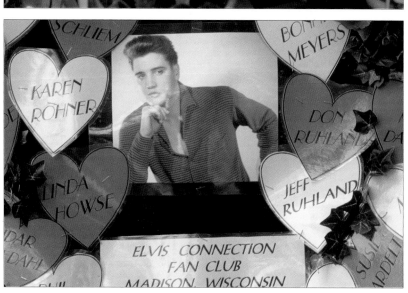

**Still
a star…**
The floral tributes
from fans are
often extremely
elaborate and
some are hand-
crafted.
Inset: Elvis
Presley's star on
the Walk of Fame
in Hollywood.

The original memorial from Gladys Presley's grave in Forest Hill Cemetery, with the Italian statue specially commissioned by Elvis and Vernon just after her death.
Opposite top: The name and image of Elvis lives on around the world.
Opposite bottom: Elvis's childhood home in Tupelo is now a tourist attraction – although it is furnished with home comforts the Presley's could never have afforded when they lived there.

The 1928 Kimball grand piano that Priscilla gave Elvis as an anniversary present, and which she had covered in 24-carat gold leaf both inside and out. It was first placed in the music room at Graceland but is now displayed at Nashville's Country Music Hall of Fame.

Opposite top: Elvis bought this pink Cadillac sedan for Gladys in 1956 – despite the fact she could not drive. It was the only Cadillac that he kept throughout his life and he promised it to Lisa Marie on her 18th birthday.

Opposite bottom: The living room at Graceland has been kept very much as Elvis left it and the décor and furnishings are flamboyant. The stained glass peacock was specially designed for the room – although displaying peacock feathers indoors is supposed to bring bad luck.

BIBLIOGRAPHY

Elvis Presley: The King of Rock 'n' Roll, Robert Daily, New York: Franklin Watts, 1996

Elvis: Portrait of the King, Susan Doll, Illinois: Publications International, Ltd, 1995

Last Train to Memphis, Peter Guralnik, London: Abacus, 1994

Careless Love, Peter Guralnik, London: Abacus, 1999

Elvis Aaron Presley: Revelations from the Memphis Mafia, Alana Nash (with Billy Smith, Marty Lacker and Lamar Fike), London: HarperCollins, 1995

The Ultimate Elvis, Patricia Jobe Pierce, New York: Simon & Schuster, 1994

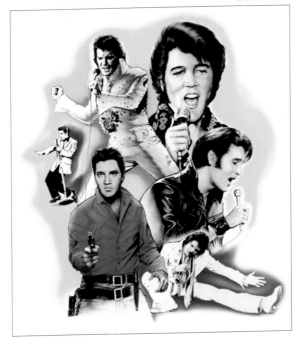

FACTS AND FIGURES

Elvis Presley has sold an estimated one billion records worldwide –
more than anyone else in record industry history.

Certified gold and platinum records in the USA alone, based on current sales
standards of half a million for gold and one million for platinum, are as follows:

32 gold albums

32 platinum albums

24 gold singles

27 platinum singles

6 gold EP singles

10 platinum EP singles

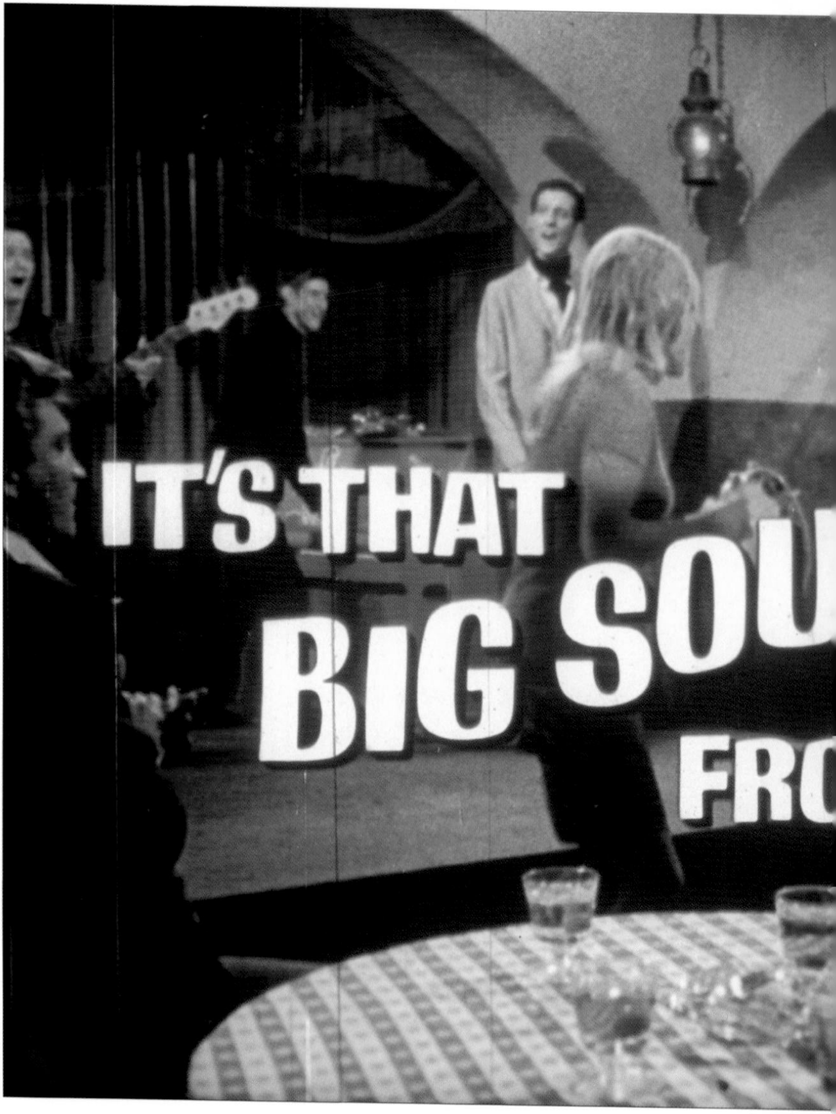
IT'S THAT
BIG SOU
FRO

Elvis's chart career looks like this:

- 149 songs in the *Billboard* Hot 100

- 18 songs made No. 1 in the *Billboard* Hot 100

- 9 albums made No. 1 in the *Billboard* Top 100 album chart

He has also received a host of awards and nominations:

- 14 Grammy nominations from the National Academy of Recording Arts and Sciences (NARAS)

- 3 Grammy awards

- 4 recordings in the NARAS Hall of Fame

Elvis has also played a major role on-screen, with:

- 31 feature films as an actor

- 2 concert documentary films made during his lifetime

- 11 film soundtrack albums, which made the top ten of the *Billboard* Top 100 album chart

- *Elvis: Aloha From Hawaii*, seen in 40 countries by 1–1.5 billion people, and in more American homes than man's first steps on the moon.

Elvis played nearly 1,100 concerts between 1969 and 1977.

His charitable donations include the following:

- raised over $65,000 towards the building of the USS *Arizona* Memorial at Pearl Harbor with a benefit concert in Hawaii

- raised $75,000 for the Kui Lee Cancer Fund in Hawaii, from sales of audience tickets for rehearsals for the *Aloha From Hawaii* TV special

- for many years, Elvis gave $1,000 annually to each of 50 Memphis charities.

Elvis's home, Graceland, attracts over 600,000 visitors a year and is the most famous American home after the White House.

The first Elvis postage stamp had a print run of 500 million – three times the normal number for a commemorative stamp.

Elvis is the only person who is currently a member of three US Halls of Fame: Rock and Roll, Country and Gospel.

There are still over 625 active Elvis fanclubs worldwide.

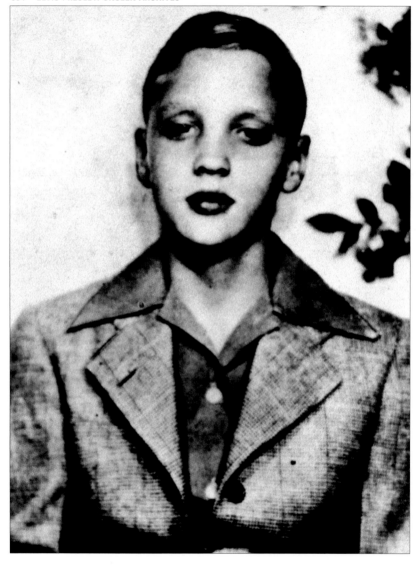

CHRONOLOGY
1933 – 2002

1933

17 Jun   Gladys Love Smith and Vernon Elvis Presley are married

1935

8 Jan   Elvis Aaron Presley is born at his parents' home, 306 Old Saltillo Road; his twin brother, Jesse Garon Presley, is stillborn

1937

10 Nov   Vernon Presley is found guilty of forging a cheque

1938

25 May   Vernon Presley is sentenced to serve three years at Parchman penal plantation, a Mississippi state penitentiary, and Gladys and Elvis are left to live on welfare

1940

10 Oct   Vernon is released from prison early because of good behaviour

1945

8 Jan   Elvis receives his first guitar for his tenth birthday

3 Oct   At the annual Mississippi–Alabama Fair and Dairy Show, held in Tupelo, Mississippi, Elvis sings 'Old Shep' in a live competition and wins second-place prize of five dollars and free admission to the fairground rides

1948

Aug   Governor Jimmie 'Pappy' Davis of Louisiana bestows the honorary title of 'Colonel' on his friend Tom Parker

12 Sept   The Presleys move overnight to Memphis, after Vernon is caught trucking for a bootlegger and is fired from his job

1949

20 Sept   The Presleys move into federal-funded accommodation in Memphis and life becomes more stable for nearly three years

1951

3 Jun   Elvis starts work at Precision Tools

1 Jul   Elvis is fired when it is learned that he is under-age

1952

Mar   Elvis plays at the Palm Club on Summer Avenue, Memphis, but the gig goes unnoticed

24 Dec   Elvis sings 'Old Shep' and 'Cold, Cold Icy Fingers' at his school's Christmas concert to rave reviews

1953

8 Jan   Vernon and Gladys pay $50 for a 1942 Lincoln Zephyr coupé, as an 18th-birthday present for Elvis

9 Apr   At the 'Annual Minstrel' at his school, Elvis sings a blues version of 'Keep Them Icy Fingers Off of Me'; he receives an encore and sings a second song, which was either "Til I Waltz Again With You' or 'Old Shep'

26 May   After hitchhiking to Meridian, Mississippi, Elvis sings at the First Jimmie Rodgers Memorial Talent Show at the Lamar Hotel and wins the second-place guitar prize with a country version of 'I'm Left, You're Right, She's Gone' and a rock version of 'Baby, Let's Play House'

3 Jun   Elvis graduates from Class 202 at Humes High School

Summer   Elvis records 'My Happiness' and 'That's When Your Heartache Begins' at Sam Phillips's Memphis Recording Service; he takes the original pressing and no copies are made

1954

4 Jan   Elvis records 'I'll Never Stand In Your Way' and 'Casual Love Affair' at Sam Phillips's Memphis Recording Service; again, he takes the original pressing and no copies are made

Jan   Dixie Locke becomes Elvis's first serious girlfriend

May   Sam Phillips asks Elvis to sing 'Without You', but is not impressed; however, he calls guitarist Scotty Moore and bass player Bill Black, and asks them to work with Elvis; the three rehearse for weeks at Phillips's Sun Studios

Jul   Elvis gives his first interview, to editor Paul Ackerman of *Billboard*

Jul   At the Bon Air Club, Memphis, Elvis sings 'That's All Right, Mama' and 'Blue Moon of Kentucky', backed by Doug Poindexter and the Starlight Wranglers, with Scotty Moore and Bill Black

5–6 Jul   Elvis, Scotty Moore and Bill Black record 'That's All Right, Mama' and 'Blue Moon of Kentucky' at Sun Studios

7 Jul   Sam Phillips sends out DJ demos of the first record, and Dewey Phillips plays 'That's All Right, Mama' on WHBQ 14 times in a row; later that evening, Elvis is interviewed on-air

11 Jul   Elvis, Scotty Moore and Bill Black, along with Johnny Bernero on drums, record 'Mystery Train' at Sun Studios

12 Jul   Elvis and his parents sign a one-year contract with Scotty Moore

19 Jul   Official release of the first record 'That's All Right, Mama'/'Blue Moon Of Kentucky', which quickly sells 20,000 copies

28 Jul   The first published interview with Elvis appears in 'The Front Row' in the *Press-Scimitar*

30 Jul   Elvis appears in his first major concert, at the Overton Park Shell

7 Aug   *Billboard* reviews 'That's All Right, Mama', giving it a good write-up

Aug–Oct   Elvis and the Blue Moon Boys perform several times in Texas and at the Eagle's Nest, Memphis whenever they can

9 Sept   Marion Keisker of Sun Studios organizes a Memphis fanclub for Elvis and the Blue Moon Boys

25 Sept   Elvis and the Blue Moon Boys appear at Nashville's Grand Ole Opry, but do not go down well; Elvis never performed there again

25 Sept   Release of 'Good Rockin' Tonight'/'I Don't Care If The Sun Don't Shine'

Oct   Promoter Oscar 'The Baron' Davis brings Elvis to the attention of his boss, Colonel Tom Parker; the Colonel comes to see him perform and they meet for the first time, at Taylor's restaurant, along with Scotty, Bill Black, the Baron and Bob Neal

16 Oct	Elvis and the Blue Moon Boys appear on a radio show, the Louisiana Hayride, which went out across the southern US on KWKH from Shreveport's Municipal Auditorium; he is an instant success
23 Oct	Elvis and the Blue Moon Boys perform again at the Louisiana Hayride
Nov	The DJs at *Billboard* put Elvis eighth on a list of most promising new hillbilly or country and western singers of 1954
6 Nov	Elvis and the Blue Moon Boys perform at the Louisiana Hayride and afterwards sign a one-year contract to appear every Saturday night
Nov	The band goes on a concert tour through Texas, appearing at Boston, Lufkin, Longview, Odessa and the Memphis Airport Inn
Dec	Elvis and the Blue Moon Boys appear each week on the Louisiana Hayride show
10 Dec	Elvis records 'Milkcow Blues Boogie' at Sun Records
18 Dec	'I'm Left, You're Right, She's Gone' and a version of 'My Baby's Gone' are recorded at Sun Studios

1955

1 Jan	The OK Group of New Orleans, Louisiana, hires Elvis for one-night performances on the radio at $300 a time
8 Jan	'Milkcow Blues Boogie'/'You're A Heartbreaker' is released, but does not chart
Jan	Colonel Parker sends Jimmy Rodgers Snow, Hank Williams's son, to see Elvis perform; he reports back that Elvis is provocative, sexy and appeals to all women
Jan	Elvis and the band appear at a series of concerts in Mississippi, Arkansas, Alabama and Missouri
16 Jan	Elvis and the band appear at a concert in Booneville, Mississippi, part of which is broadcast by WBIP. Further concerts follow at Eagle's Nest, Houston and Lake Pontchartrain, New Orleans
Feb	Colonel Parker attempts to get RCA interested in Elvis, but although Steve Sholes, RCA's man in Nashville, is interested, the record company is not
Feb	Elvis and the band continue to appear at the Louisiana Hayride on Saturday nights and also play concerts in Carlsbad, New Mexico, Albuquerque, Texas, Louisiana, Arkansas and Cleveland
Mar	The band flies to New York City to audition for Arthur Godfrey's Talent Scouts, but is turned down
5 Mar	Elvis makes his TV debut when the Louisiana Hayride is broadcast regionally from Shreveport, Louisiana
Mar	Elvis and the boys appear in concerts in Tennessee, Louisiana, Arkansas, Mississippi and Missouri
19 Mar	Elvis appears live on the *Grand Prize Saturday Night Jamboree*, broadcast from Eagle's Hall in Houston, Texas, by KPRC-TV; he also records 'I Got A Woman' at the same venue
28 Mar	Part of a performance at the Circle Theater in Cleveland is broadcast on WERE radio
1 Apr	'Baby, Let's Play House'/'I'm Left, You're Right, She's Gone' is released; the A-side causes a stir as it appears to hint at pre-marital sex
16 Apr	Elvis performs for KRLD radio in Dallas, Texas
1 May	Elvis performs in New Orleans and then begins a three-week tour through Chattanooga with Hank Snow's All-Star Jamboree

13 May	Screaming teenage girls mob Elvis wherever he appears, and a concert in Jacksonville, Florida, causes a riot, with girls jumping onto the stage and trying to tear off his clothes, knocking police guards to the ground and trying to enter Elvis's dressing room
25 May	Elvis performs at the Jimmie Rodgers Memorial Day Celebration in Meridian, Mississippi
31 May	An afternoon concert in Midland, Texas is followed by a live radio appearance on *The Roy Orbison Show* in Odessa
26 Jun	After a concert in Biloxi, Mississippi, Elvis meets June Juanico, whom he dates on and off for a year
Jul	'Baby, Let's Play House' makes it into the *Billboard* Top Ten
25 Jul	A famous picture of Elvis in a gold lamé tuxedo is taken by William S Randolph at a concert in the 116th Field Artillery Armory in Tampa, Florida
6 Aug	Release of 'I Forgot To Remember To Forget'/'Mystery Train', which later goes into the *Billboard* country chart for 40 weeks
15 Aug	Elvis signs a contract giving Colonel Parker the right to manage his career, although he is still bound to Bob Neal for another year
	'Mystery Train' enters the *Billboard* country chart, staying there for 30 weeks
8 Sept	Without Colonel Parker's knowledge, Elvis signs a new contract with the Louisiana Hayride for a further year from 8 November; his payment increases from $18 a night to $200
Oct	Atlantic Records bids $25,000 for Elvis to sign with them, but is turned down
10 Nov	At the annual DJ convention in Nashville, Elvis secures the recording rights to 'Heartbreak Hotel' from Mae Axton

13 Nov	The Country and Western Disc Jockey Association names Elvis Most Promising Country Artist
19 Nov	Colonel Parker, Elvis and Red West fly to New York City to meet Jean and Julian Aberbach of Hill and Range Music
20 Nov	Sun Records' contract with Elvis is bought for $25,000 by RCA Victor, while Hill and Range Music buys Sam Phillips's Hi-Lo music publishing company for $15,000
Nov	Elvis and Dixie Locke break up, as his new life keeps them apart too much
22 Nov	Elvis signs a contract making Colonel Parker his exclusive representative

1956

5 Jan	Colonel Parker does a deal with Hill and Range Music, establishing a 50/50 partnership for five years with the newly created Presley Music Inc to publish the songs Elvis records
9 Jan	Elvis rehearses 'Heartbreak Hotel' before recording it for RCA the following day, along with 'I Got A Woman'; the next day, he records 'I Was The One' and 'I'm Counting On You'
15 Jan	RCA gives Elvis a new convertible
17 Jan	Release of 'Heartbreak Hotel'/'I Was The One'
28 Jan	Elvis appears on Milton Berle's *Stage Show* on CBS TV. This was the first of several TV appearances including the Dorsey Brothers' Stage Show and Ella Fitzgerald's *Stage Show*.
30/31 Jan	'Blue Suede Shoes' is recorded during a two-day studio session
15 Feb	'I Forgot To Remember To Forget'/'Mystery Train' both reach No. 1 on the *Billboard* country chart, the first Elvis records to do so

22 Feb	'Heartbreak Hotel' enters the *Billboard* Top 100 at No. 68 and the Country's Best Sellers in Stores chart at No. 9
29 Feb	'I Was The One' enters the *Billboard* Top 100 at No. 84
1 Mar	RCA is overwhelmed with 362,000 advance orders for the first LP, 'Elvis Presley'
3 Mar	RCA's Top 25 Best Sellers list contains six records by Elvis

7 Mar	'Heartbreak Hotel' is No. 1 on the *Billboard* Country Best Sellers in Stores chart
13 Mar	Release of the LP, 'Elvis Presley', which goes on to become the first in history to sell a million copies and stays in the *Billboard* extended-play album chart for a total of 68 weeks
15 Mar	Colonel Parker becomes the sole official manager of Elvis

17 Mar	Elvis appears on the St Patrick's Day *Stage Show* on CBS TV
28 Mar	'Blue Suede Shoes' enters the *Billboard* Top 100 chart at No. 88
1 Apr	Elvis does a screen-test in Los Angeles for Hal Wallis of Paramount Pictures
Apr	'Heartbreak Hotel' is No. 1 on the *Billboard* pop chart and stays there for seven weeks; at the same time it is No. 1 on the country and western chart and No. 5 on the R&B chart
6 Apr	Paramount Pictures signs Elvis to a seven-year, three-movie contract
May	Release of 'I Want You, I Need You, I Love You', which stays in the *Billboard* Top 100 for 24 weeks and reaches No. 3, also getting to No. 10 on the R&B chart and No. 1 for one week on the country chart; the flipside was 'My Baby Left Me'
11 Apr	*Variety* claims that 'Heartbreak Hotel' has become the first Presley record to sell a million copies
23 Apr	Elvis begins a four-week engagement at the New Frontier Hotel, Las Vegas, but the audience does not respond well to him and he only stays for two weeks
Apr	Elvis has talks with Liberace, who becomes a major influence on how he dresses and presents himself
Jun	RCA releases the LP 'Elvis Presley', which goes on to stay in the *Billboard* Top 100 for 12 weeks, reaching No. 24
Jun	*Time* nicknames Elvis 'The Pelvis'
1 Jul	Elvis appears on *The Steve Allen Show*, singing 'Hound Dog' to a basset hound
20 Aug	Elvis begins filming *Love Me Tender* in Hollywood for Twentieth Century Fox
3 Sept	Although she does not drive, Elvis buys his mother Gladys a pink Cadillac
5 Sept	'Don't Be Cruel'/'Hound Dog' reaches

	No. 1 on the *Billboard* Top 100
9 Sept	*The Ed Sullivan Show* gets the highest ratings in television history when Elvis appears
19 Sept	'Blue Moon' enters the *Billboard* Top 100 at No. 87
Sept	In an interview in the *New York Daily News*, Elvis says there should be no draft, which encourages some young men to burn their draft cards
Sept	Release of 'Tryin' To Get To You'/'I Love You Because', 'Blue Suede Shoes'/'Tutti Frutti' and 'One-Sided Love Affair'/'Money Honey', none of which chart
25 Sept	Rumors circulate that Elvis is romancing actress Debra Paget, and that they will marry
26 Sept	Tupelo inaugurates Elvis Presley Day
30 Sept	Cardinal Spellman speaks out against Elvis, and Gladys is distraught to hear her son condemned
Oct	Variety names Elvis 'King of Rock 'n' Roll' and he also appears on the cover of *Rock and Roll* magazine
Oct	Elvis receives his draft questionnaire
3 Oct	'I Don't Care If The Sun Don't Shine' enters the *Billboard* Top 100 at No. 77
8 Oct	*Time* reveals that RCA has advance orders of one million for the single 'Love Me Tender' – an all-time high
10 Oct	'Love Me Tender'/'Any Way You Want Me' enters the *Billboard* Top 100 at No. 9
18 Oct	Elvis gets into a fight with a gas station owner, who asks him to leave after his Cadillac draws a crowd of fans nearly causing a riot
19 Oct	The LP 'Elvis' is released
24 Oct	Elvis earns a gold record for 'Love Me Tender', his fifth of the year

27 Oct   The front page of *Billboard* announces that the Army plans to give Elvis a GI haircut, which causes fans to panic

31 Oct   Elvis starts to date Barbara Hearn

Nov   The LPs 'Elvis Vol 1' and 'Elvis Vol 2' are released

7 Nov   'Love Me' enters the *Billboard* Top 100 at No. 84, the LP 'Elvis' enters the Best Selling Packaged Records – Popular Albums at No. 7, and 'Love Me Tender' reaches No. 1 on the Top 100

14 Nov   At a Liberace concert in the Riviera Hotel, Las Vegas, Elvis is in the audience and after the show the two of them exchange jackets

15 Nov   The movie *Love Me Tender* opens in 500 cinemas across the States and is a smash hit

21 Nov   Colonel Parker owns Elvis completely, after he gets Bob Neal to sign a contract to that effect, and pays off Hank Snow in lieu of a finder's fee

23 Nov   Louis Balint, an unemployed steelworker, is fined $19.60 for attacking Elvis because his wife's passion for the singer had broken up their marriage

28 Nov   The film *Love Me Tender* enters *Variety's* National Box Office Survey at No. 2

Dec   Release of the LP 'Love Me Tender'

15 Dec   Elvis appears at the Louisiana Hayride for the last time

Dec   'Heartbreak Hotel' is the *Billboard* No. 1 single for 1956

1957

4 Jan   Accompanied by Las Vegas dancer Dorothy Harmony, Elvis has his pre-induction Army physical at Kennedy Veterans Hospital

6 Jan   Elvis appears for the final time on *The Ed Sullivan Show*

Jan   The Army announces that Elvis is classed 1-A for draft

21 Jan   Start of the filming of *Loving You*, for Paramount

Jan   Release of 'Too Much'/'Playing For Keeps', which stays in the *Billboard* Top 100 for 17 weeks, at No. 2 for four of them

5 Mar   Gladys and Vernon Presley see Graceland and persuade Elvis that he should buy it

7 Mar   Elvis pays $102,500 for Graceland, far outbidding an offer of $35,000 from the YMCA

Mar   RCA gives Elvis a suit made of gold lamé, from Nudie's Rodeo Tailors in Hollywood which he wears for the first time at a concert in Kiel Auditorium, St Louis

10 Apr   'All Shook Up' reaches No. 1 on the *Billboard* Top 100 and stays there for eight weeks

13 May   Start of shooting on *Jailhouse Rock* for MGM, in Culver City

14 May   After swallowing the porcelain cap from one of his teeth, Elvis is rushed to the Cedars of Lebanon Hospital, California, with chest pains

June   'Teddy Bear'/'Loving You' is the first Elvis single to be distributed in the UK, and sells over a million copies

9 Jul   Premiere of *Loving You* at the Strand Theater in Memphis

27 Jul   'Teddy Bear'/'Loving You' hits No. 1 on the *Billboard* Top 100 and stays there for 17 weeks, it is also at No. 1 for one week on both the R&B and the country charts

30 Aug   According to a report in *The Spokane Review* the following day, Elvis whips 12,000 fans into frenzy at a concert in the Memorial Stadium in Spokane, Washington; fans try to steal soil from the infield, because his feet have touched it

Sept	The single 'Jailhouse Rock'/'Treat Me Nice' is released in the UK and becomes the first Elvis record to enter the charts at No. 1 in England; it has already been released in the US and goes on to sell over three million copies in 12 months
Sept	Scotty Moore and Bill Black leave Elvis because of their poor pay and lack of recognition, although they play at some further recording sessions
27 Sept	At Tupelo's Mississippi–Alabama Fair and Dairy Show, Elvis plays at a concert to benefit the Elvis Presley Youth Recreation Center, which he goes on to establish in his home town that December
28 Sept	The LP 'Elvis Presley' reaches No. 1 on the *Billboard* extended-play album chart and stays there for six weeks
17 Oct	Premiere of *Jailhouse Rock* in Memphis
8 Nov	*Jailhouse Rock* opens across the country and goes on to make a profit within three weeks
19 Dec	Elvis receives his draft notice

1958

Jan	Release of 'I Beg Of You', which stays in the *Billboard* Top 100 for 12 weeks, reaching No. 12, and getting to No. 4 on the R&B chart and No. 2 on the country chart
5 Mar	Filming starts on *King Creole* for Paramount and later moves to New Orleans
10 Mar	End of filming on *King Creole*
24 Mar	Elvis is inducted into the Army and is sent to Fort Chaffee, Arkansas
25 Mar	An Army haircut removes his famous ducktail hairstyle and sideburns
28 Mar	Elvis is sent to Fort Hood with his battalion for basic training

1 May	After the Colonel discovers that a soldier can live off-base if he has dependants in the area, Elvis moves his parents, along with his grandmother and Lamar Fike, into a rented house nearby and drives into base every day for duty
June	Since her health has been failing for some time, Gladys returns to Memphis for treatment
1 Jul	*King Creole* is released to good reviews
5 Aug	Gladys is taken into the hospital and Elvis is granted compassionate leave to visit her
11 Aug	Elvis receives his first RIAA Gold Disc Award for 'Hard-Headed Woman'
14 Aug	Gladys dies of a heart attack in the hospital
16 Aug	Gladys's funeral is held in Memphis and she is buried at Forest Hill Cemetery
24 Aug	As his unit is soon being sent to Germany, Elvis returns to basic training
19 Sept	With his Army unit, Elvis travels from Fort Hood to Brooklyn, New York
22 Sept	Elvis and his unit leave on the USS *General Randall* for Bremerhaven, Germany, where they disembark to transfer to Friedberg
10 Oct	The entourage moves into a rented house, and Elvis moves off base to join them
23 Oct	Bill Haley and the Comets play a concert in Frankfurt, which Elvis attends, posing afterwards in Haley's dressing room
Nov	Elvis goes on manoeuvres along the Czech border
1 Nov	Elvis is dubbed 'public enemy number one' by Russian leaders; actress Venetia Stevenson flies to Germany to see Elvis

27 Nov	Elvis is promoted to private first class
20 Dec	After buying a used BMW 507 sports car from the company, Elvis agrees to pose for publicity shots
Dec	Elvis is named World's Outstanding Popular Singer, World's Outstanding Musical Personality, and Favourite US Male Singer for 1958

1959

Jan	Robert Stephen Marquett, the son of an Army master sergeant, is pictured with Elvis and the photo becomes a 1959 March of Dimes poster
1 Jan	Vernon crashes his son's black Mercedes into a tree, and in the confusion the German newspapers report that Elvis has been killed; Vernon is unhurt, but his passenger, a young secretary, is paralysed for a short period
8 Jan	On his 24th birthday, Elvis is called by Dick Clark, who tells him he has been voted Best Singer of the Year, and that 'King Creole' is Best Song of the Year; that evening, Dick Clark's *American Bandstand* programme is dedicated to Elvis
3 Feb	Elvis is deeply upset by the death of Buddy Holly, Ritchie Valens and Jiles Perry Richardson (the Big Bopper), along with their pilot, in a plane crash; all the musicians were friends
Apr	A war memorial is erected in Steinfurth by Elvis and his Army unit
May	In Friedberg, Elvis briefly dates Janie Wilbanks
1 Jun	Elvis is promoted to specialist fourth class
3–9 Jun	Elvis gets tonsillitis and is sent to Frankfurt Military Hospital
21 Jun	Elvis and his entourage charter a plane and fly to Paris, where they stay at the Prince de Galles hotel on Avenue Georges V and frequent all the famous nightclubs
24–29 Oct	Elvis gets tonsillitis again and is sent to the General Hospital in Frankfurt
Nov	Priscilla Beaulieu is introduced to Elvis at a party
Nov	Vernon meets Dee Stanley, an American in Germany with her husband and family
Nov	After having karate lessons from Jurgen Seydel, Elvis has his photo taken in karate gi with a white belt
Dec	The magazine *Elvis Monthly* is published in the UK by Albert Hand
25 Dec	Elvis takes Priscilla to local festivities and meets her parents

1960

20 Jan	Elvis is promoted to sergeant
Feb	The magazine *Elvis Monthly* is released in the US
17 Feb	The RIAA finally certifies the LP 'Elvis' a Gold Disc – although it has already sold more than three million copies
Mar	A 'Letter from Elvis' is printed in *Photoplay* and he appears in Army fatigues on the cover
Mar	*TV Radio Mirror* holds a contest to see who should be King of Rock 'n' Roll and Elvis is voted the winner
2 Mar	Elvis leaves Germany from Wiesbaden airport and arrives the following day at McGuire Air Force Base at Fort Dix
3 Mar	A photo of Elvis in uniform is featured on the front pages of newspapers across America; after being discharged, the ex-soldier tells the press there is no one special in his life and that he wants to concentrate on acting rather than singing. He then goes straight into the recording studio to produce some new songs

23 Mar	Travelling by train to Miami, the railway track is lined with fans and photographers trying to get a glimpse of Elvis
3 Apr	Release of the LP 'Elvis Is Back', which goes on to stay in the *Billboard* chart for 56 weeks, at No. 2 for three of them
3 Apr	'It's Now Or Never'/'A Mess Of Blues' is recorded, going on to enter the *Billboard* Hot 100 at No. 44 and climbing to No. 1 within five weeks; it remains in the chart for 20 weeks, also reaching No. 7 on the R&B chart, and becomes the *Billboard* Vocal Single of 1960; it carries on selling through the years, achieving sales of well over 23 million copies
4 Apr	'Are You Lonesome Tonight' is recorded and makes the largest chart leap so far, entering the *Billboard* Hot 100 at No. 35 but jumping to No. 2 within seven days; it stays in the chart for 16 weeks, also reaching No. 22 on the country chart, No. 3 on the R&B chart and staying at No. 1 in the English charts for four weeks
1 May	Elvis and his entourage arrive at the Beverly Wilshire to begin filming on *GI Blues* for Paramount
12 May	*The Frank Sinatra – Timex Special*, featuring Elvis and recorded at the Fontainbleau Hotel in Miami Beach, is broadcast on 12 May on ABC TV, and also includes a host of other stars, including Nancy Sinatra, Sammy Davis Jr and Peter Lawford
13 May	The change of style as featured on the Sinatra show upsets many fans; some critics accuse Elvis of deserting rock 'n' roll, or becoming lazy and no longer caring about the music, although others feel he has matured
Jun	*Movie Mirror* announces that 'The King of Rock 'n' Roll is Dead!' and reports that Elvis is now conservative
Jun	During a trip to Las Vegas, Elvis's entourage is christened the 'Memphis Mafia'; the name sticks
3 Jul	Vernon marries Dee Stanley, but Elvis refuses to attend the wedding
20 Jul	Vernon brings Dee and her three sons to Graceland, but they soon move out again to a house on Dolan Avenue
15 Aug	Filming begins on *Flaming Star* for Twentieth Century Fox
18 Aug	Preview of *GI Blues*, which becomes a big box-office draw, despite being disliked by the critics
Sept	The Mexican government bans all Elvis movies after a showing of *GI Blues* in Mexico City causes a riot
4 Oct	Filming finishes on *Flaming Star* and Elvis embarks on a short-lived affair with wardrobe assistant Nancy Sharp
30 Oct	'It's Now Or Never'/'A Mess Of Blues' goes in at No. 1 in the English charts, and stays there for eight weeks
11 Nov	Filming begins on *Wild in the Country* for Twentieth Century Fox
23 Nov	National release of *GI Blues*, which reaches No. 2 in *Variety's* list of top-grossing movies
23 Nov	A version of *Flaming Star* with only two songs is previewed in Westchester, California; it is later selected for general release and goes into *Variety's* list of top-grossing movies at No. 12. A version of the movie with four songs is previewed, but is later dropped
Dec	Elvis is inducted into the Los Angeles Indian Tribal Council by Chief Wah-Nee-Ota

1961

3 Jan	Elvis returns to Los Angeles to finish filming on *Wild in the Country*
8 Jan	On the set of *Wild in the Country*, Elvis

celebrates his birthday with actress Hope Lange

18 Jan Filming finishes on *Wild in the Country*

8 Mar Governor Buford Ellington bestows the honorary title of 'Colonel' on Elvis

14 Mar Elvis flies to California with his entourage to begin filming on *Blue Hawaii* for Paramount

24 Mar Elvis flies to Hawaii

25 Mar A charity concert for the USS *Arizona* Memorial Fund, held at Bloch Arena in Pearl Harbor, Hawaii, raises $65,000

15 Jun *Wild in the Country* is premiered, then released nationwide

1 Jul The wedding of Red West and Patricia Boyd is attended by Elvis with Anita Wood

6–7 Jul Elvis and his entourage travel by bus from Nashville to Florida

11 Jul Filming begins on Follow *That Dream* for United Artists

Sept–Oct Elvis spends some time in Hollywood, briefly flying to Nashville to record more songs

5–14 Nov Elvis is coached for the boxing scenes in *Kid Galahad* by former junior welterweight champion Mush Callahan

Nov Filming begins on *Kid Galahad* for United Artists

21 Nov *Blue Hawaii* is released nationally and, by the end of the year, has grossed $4.7 million

30 Nov Elvis is offered the lead in *Too Late Blues*, but the Colonel makes him turn it down

1962

8 Jan Dick Clark dedicates the broadcast of *American Bandstand* to Elvis on his birthday

Feb Colonel Parker persuades Elvis to turn down the part of Chance Wayne in *Sweet Bird of Youth*, the film of Tennessee Williams's play; the role goes to Paul Newman instead

7 Apr Elvis flies to Hawaii to begin filming on *Girls! Girls! Girls!* for Paramount

11 Apr Premiere of *Follow That Dream* in Ocala, Florida

15 May The cast and crew return to Culver City to complete filming

23 May National release of *Follow That Dream*, which did not do well at the box office

June After protracted negotiations with her stepfather, Priscilla Beaulieu arrives in Los Angeles from Germany to spend some time with Elvis

27 Aug Filming begins on *It Happened at the World's Fair* for MGM

29 Aug National release of *Kid Galahad*, which goes on to gross $1.7 million by the end of the year

8 Sept Elvis arrives in Seattle for further filming on *It Happened at the World's Fair*, staying at the New Washington Hotel

Oct Release of 'Return To Sender'/'Where Do You Come From?', which reaches No. 2 on the *Billboard* Hot 100, No. 5 on the R&B chart and was No. 1 for three weeks in the UK

31 Oct Premiere of *Girls! Girls! Girls!* in Honolulu

Nov Elvis returns to Graceland for three weeks

21 Nov National release of Girls! Girls! Girls!, which goes on to gross $2.6 million by the end of the year

Dec Elvis is voted fifth top box-office draw by cinema owners and receives three Norwegian Silver Record Awards for 'Good Luck Charm'

| Dec | Priscilla's parents are persuaded to let her come to America to spend Christmas with Elvis at Graceland |

1963

Jan	Priscilla returns to Germany, but Elvis asks her stepfather if she can move to America and finish her education at a private school in Memphis
28 Jan	Filming begins on *Fun in Acapulco* for Paramount; although some shots were done in Acapulco, Elvis only filmed in Hollywood on Paramount's lots
5 Mar	Elvis is badly upset when his friend Patsy Cline, touring companion Lloyd 'Cowboy' Copas, and Harold 'Hawkshaw' Hawkins are killed in a plane crash
15 Mar	Filming is completed on *Fun in Acapulco*
Mar	Priscilla moves into Graceland with her parents' permission and is enrolled at the Immaculate Conception High School, an all-girls Catholic establishment
3 Apr	Premiere of *It Happened at the World's Fair* in Los Angeles
10 Apr	Nationwide opening of *It Happened at the World's Fair*, which goes on to gross $2.25 million by the end of the year
29 May	Priscilla graduates from the Immaculate Conception High School
15 Jul	Filming begins on *Viva Las Vegas* for MGM; during the filming Elvis and his co-star Ann-Margret have an affair
5 Oct	Filming begins on *Kissin' Cousins* for MGM
21 Oct	Filming finishes on *Kissin' Cousins*
27 Nov	National release of *Fun in Acapulco*, which goes on to gross over $1.5 million by the end of the year
11 Dec	*Love Me Tender* is shown on television

| Dec | Elvis is voted seventh top box-office draw by cinema owners |

1964

1 Jan	Elvis is rejected in favour of George Hamilton to play Hank Williams in the movie of his life, *Your Cheatin' Heart*, because Williams's widow feels the presence of Elvis would overshadow her husband's story
30 Jan	The yacht *Potomac*, which had once been owned by President Franklin D Roosevelt, is bought by Elvis
Feb	Movie Life runs an article about Elvis marrying Ann-Margret, but it refers to their screen wedding in *Viva Las Vegas*
7 Feb	The Beatles arrive in New York and Elvis sends them a congratulatory telegram
15 Feb	Elvis donates the yacht *Potomac* to St Jude's Children's Hospital
Feb–Mar	*Kissin' Cousins* has sneak previews in North Long Beach, California and Phoenix, Arizona
9 Mar	Filming begins on *Roustabout* for Paramount
11 Mar	An award for Americanism is given to Elvis by Shelby County and Memphis business leaders
Apr	*Kissin' Cousins* opens across the nation
Apr	First publication of the newspaper *The Elvis Echo*, edited by Paulette Sansone
20 Apr	Premiere of *Viva Las Vegas* in New York; filming finishes on *Roustabout*
30 Apr	Elvis and Larry Geller meet for the first time when Geller comes to cut Elvis's hair; Geller persuades Elvis to study the occult
17 Jun	National release of *Viva Las Vegas*, which goes on to gross over $4.5 million by the end of the year
22 Jun	Filming begins on *Girl Happy* for MGM

Jul   Elvis receives a South African Gold Record Award for 'Kiss Me Quick' on the MGM lot of *Girl Happy*

1 Aug   Johnny Burnette, a close friend of Elvis's, is drowned in California; Elvis is devastated

Aug   The UK press report that Ann-Margret and Elvis plan to marry, although she denies saying anything

6 Oct   Filming begins on Tickle Me for Allied Artists

11 Nov   National release of *Roustabout*, which goes on to gross $3 million by the end of the year

Dec   Elvis is voted sixth top box-office draw by cinema owners and is presented with an award as Tennessee's Entertainer of the Year

1965

8 Jan   Elvis celebrates his 30th birthday at Graceland

15 Mar   Filming begins on *Harum Scarum* for MGM

Apr   Elvis starts to visit the Self-Realization Fellowship Center and later meets its president, Sri Daya Mata

14 Apr   National release of *Girl Happy*, which goes on to gross $3.1 million by the end of the year, despite poor reviews

25 May	Filming begins on *Frankie and Johnny* for United Artists
28 May	Premiere of *Tickle Me* in Atlanta, Georgia
7 Aug	Filming begins on *Paradise, Hawaiian Style*
9/10 Aug	Elvis is absent without explanation from the set of *Paradise, Hawaiian Style*
27 Aug	The Beatles and Brian Epstein meet Elvis at his Bel Air home
21 Oct	Bill Black, one of the Blue Moon Boys, dies during surgery for a brain tumour
24 Nov	Premiere of *Harum Scarum* in Los Angeles
Dec	Elvis moves from Perugia Way, Bel Air, to Rocca Place in Stone Canyon

1966

20 Feb	Filming begins on *Spinout* for MGM
Feb	President Lyndon Baines Johnson visits Elvis on the set of *Spinout*
Mar	Felton Jarvis of RCA becomes producer of Elvis's recording sessions
31 Mar	Premiere of *Frankie and Johnny* in Baton Rouge, Louisiana
6 Apr	Filming finishes on *Spinout*
May	A short promotional movie for *Paradise, Hawaiian Style* is released
Jun	Sneak previews of *Paradise, Hawaiian Style* in Memphis and New York City
11 Jun	Filming begins on *Double Trouble* for MGM
6 Jul	Nationwide release of *Paradise, Hawaiian Style*, which goes on to gross over $2.5 million by the end of the year
5 Sept	Filming finishes on *Double Trouble*
7/13 Sept	In an article, Weekend wonders if Elvis and Priscilla are secretly married

Sept	Elvis rents an ultra-modern house in Palm Springs as a private retreat
12 Sept	Filming begins on *Easy Come, Easy Go* for Paramount
13 Sept	A sneak preview of *Spinout* is attended by members of the Presley family, but not Elvis, who is still filming *Easy Come, Easy Go*
28 Oct	Filming finishes on *Easy Come, Easy Go*
1 Nov	The RIAA certifies the LP 'Elvis Presley' as a Platinum Disc after it has sold a million copies
23 Nov	Nationwide release of *Spinout*
Dec	Both her parents and the Colonel insist that it is time Elvis marries Priscilla or that she moves out of Graceland so, just before Christmas, he finally proposes
Dec	Elvis is voted tenth top box-office draw by cinema owners – it is the last time he appears in the poll

1967

9 Feb	Elvis buys the Circle G Ranch in Walls, Mississippi
Mar	Annette Day, co-star of *Double Trouble*, is given a white Mustang by Elvis
Mar	Filming begins on *Clambake* for United Artists in Los Angeles
10 Mar	After slipping in a bathroom, Elvis suffers mild concussion
22 Mar	National opening of *Easy Come, Easy Go*, which goes on to gross over $1.95 million by the end of the year
5 Apr	Nationwide release of *Double Trouble*, which soon grosses $1.6 million
1 May	Elvis marries Priscilla Beaulieu at the Aladdin Hotel, Las Vegas, in a private ceremony
2/6 May	Elvis and Priscilla honeymoon in Palm Springs, California, and then go on to

	the Circle G Ranch, accompanied by some of the Memphis Mafia
7 May	Elvis and Priscilla move to a new home in Hillcrest Road, Beverly Hills
29 May	A second wedding ceremony is held at Graceland, as many people were excluded from the first
Jun	*TV and Movie Guide* speculates that Nancy Sinatra might steal Elvis from Priscilla
12 Jun	Filming begins on *Speedway* for MGM, which also stars Nancy Sinatra
Jun	An article in *Screen Stories* suggests that Nancy Sinatra and Elvis are romantically involved
8 Sept	Filming finishes on *Speedway*
9 Sept	Elvis flies to Nashville, leaving Priscilla in Bel Air
18 Oct	Filming begins on *Stay Away, Joe* for MGM in Arizona
Nov	The cover of *Screen Life* features Elvis, and reports that he is to be a father
22 Nov	Release of *Clambake*, which gets mixed reviews
3 Dec	A special radio show, *Season's Greetings From Elvis*, is aired on RCA
8 Dec	TV premiere of *Tickle Me* on CBS TV's *Friday Night at the Movies*
Dec	Elvis receives a Grammy Award for Best Sacred Performance for 'How Great Thou Art'; a pop poll names him No. 1 Male Singer and No. 1 Music Personality in America
31 Dec	The Manhattan Club in Memphis is hired by Elvis for a New Year's Eve party with 500 guests, but Elvis himself does not attend

1968

Jan	Elvis announces that he wants to do a singing tour of Europe, but the plan does not come to anything
1 Feb	Lisa Marie Presley is born at the Baptist Memorial Hospital
Feb	Release of 'Elvis' Gold Records, Vol 4'
7 Feb	Nick Adams, a close friend of Elvis's, commits suicide and Elvis is deeply affected
8 Feb	*Playboy* magazine honours Elvis in its feature on the year's music scene
5 Mar	Elvis flies to California for a recording session
8 Mar	National distribution of *Stay Away, Joe*
25 May	At a karate tournament in Honolulu, Elvis meets martial arts expert Mike Stone and suggests he teaches Priscilla
May	Priscilla buys a 1928 Kimball grand piano and has it gold-leafed inside and out; she gives it to Elvis on their first wedding anniversary
15 Jun	Elvis and Priscilla fly to Honolulu to see the USS *Arizona* Memorial
Jun	*TV Times* reports that Elvis fans no longer scream when he appears
27/30 Jun	Elvis tapes a TV special for NBC TV, and is persuaded to appear in black leather and go back to his musical roots
Jul	Filming begins on *Live a Little, Love a Little* for MGM in Los Angeles
4 Jul	Elvis donates his Rolls-Royce Phantom V to a charity auction; it raises $35,000
22 Jul	Work commences on *Charro!* for National General in Arizona
30 Sept	The funeral of Dewey Phillips in Memphis, which Elvis attends
Oct	Priscilla and Elvis are featured on the cover of *Screen Life*, with an article about them wanting another baby
23 Oct	Release of *Live a Little, Love a Little*
28 Oct	Filming begins on *The Trouble with Girls* for MGM

3 Dec	The comeback TV special *Elvis* is broadcast on NBC TV and is the highest-rated programme that week
4 Dec	The *New York Times* reports that Elvis has found his way home, and fans rush to buy his records again
31 Dec	*Elvis* is shown in the UK on BBC 2

1969

10 Mar	Filming begins on *Change of Habit* for Universal and NBC in Los Angeles
13 Mar	National release of *Charro!*, which the fans love as Elvis looks handsome and rugged in a beard
Apr	Gospel singer Clara Ward and Blues singer Mahalia Jackson visit Elvis on the set of *Change of Habit*
2 May	Filming of *Change of Habit* is completed
May	Elvis decides that he no longer wants to act in movies, but would like to return to singing
21 May	The Circle G Ranch is sold and the horses moved to Graceland
1 Jun	Elvis goes on a diet to lose weight for his Las Vegas shows, before rehearsals begin in July
15 Jun	'In the Ghetto' is certified gold by the RIAA
31 Jul	At the International Hotel, Las Vegas, Elvis appears live in concert for the first time in eight years
1 Aug	Elvis tells reporters that he plans a world tour, but it does not come off
2 Aug	A gold belt is awarded to Elvis at the International Hotel for 'the world's championship attendance record'
Aug	Fans travel from all over the world to see Elvis's Vegas shows
Aug	After a press conference, *Rolling Stone* reports that Elvis is 'supernatural', *Variety* calls him a 'superstar' and

	Newsweek compliments him on his staying power
Sept	'Suspicious Minds'/'You'll Think Of Me' is released and goes into the *Billboard* Top 100 for 15 weeks, reaching No. 1 in November for one week
22 Aug	The *Elvis* TV comeback special is broadcast again
3 Sept	National release of the film *The Trouble with Girls*
10 Nov	National release of the film *Change of Habit*
12 Dec	The LP 'From Memphis to Vegas/From Vegas to Memphis' is certified gold by the RIAA

1970

21 Jan	'Don't Cry Daddy' sells a million copies and is certified gold by the RIAA
26 Jan	A new season of concerts begins at the International Hotel, Las Vegas
23 Feb	Elvis's 57th and last concert of the run at Las Vegas
27 Feb	The first concert of a three-day booking at Houston Astrodome during the Houston Livestock Show, with Elvis performing two shows a night
1 Mar	Elvis flies back to Memphis to rest; after checking into the Baptist Memorial Hospital, he is informed that he has glaucoma in his left eye
1 Jun	Felton Jarvis leaves RCA to manage Elvis's recording career
10 Aug	The first concert in a new season at the International Hotel, Las Vegas
14 Aug	A paternity suit is filed against Elvis by Patricia Parker, a Hollywood waitress; her son Jason is born on 19 October 1970
26 Aug	Threats to kidnap or kill Elvis during a show are received; the FBI is called, but it turns out to be a hoax

7 Sept	The last concert of Elvis's current Las Vegas season
8 Sept	Nancy Sinatra opens at the International Hotel, Las Vegas; Elvis, Priscilla, Vernon and Dee are in the audience; Priscilla returns home after the concert, but Elvis flies to Arizona
9 Sept	Elvis gives a concert at the Veterans Memorial Coliseum in Phoenix, Arizona, and goes on to appear in St Louis, Detroit, Miami Beach, Tampa and Mobile over the next few days
Oct	Elvis becomes a special deputy in Memphis so he can legally carry a gun
Oct	Elvis has 14-carat gold necklaces made for all the members of the Memphis Mafia, inscribed with 'TCB' (standing for Taking Care of Business) and a lightning-bolt
Nov	Elvis tells the press that his marriage has difficulties
11 Nov	The premiere of Elvis – *That's The Way It Is*, a film of concerts and recording sessions, in Phoenix, Arizona. Portland, Oregon dubs this date Elvis Presley Day, when Elvis performs at the Memorial Coliseum. During the month Elvis also gives concerts at Englewood in New Jersey, Oakland, Seattle, San Francisco, Los Angeles, San Diego, Oklahoma City and Denver
1 Dec	Elvis meets Vice President Agnew
3 Dec	Elvis spends $20,000 on guns in a three-day shopping spree
5 Dec	Elvis attends George Klein's wedding in Las Vegas, for which he has paid
21 Dec	During a meeting with President Nixon, Elvis is given a Narcotics Bureau badge since he has offered to work undercover to help stamp out drug abuse and subversive elements in America
28 Dec	At Sonny West's and Judy Morgan's wedding in Memphis, Elvis is best man, and Priscilla matron of honour
30 Dec	Elvis is taken on a tour of FBI headquarters in Washington DC

1971

9 Jan	Elvis is voted one of the Ten Outstanding Young Men of America by the Jaycees, members of the Junior Chamber of Commerce; it is to be the only award Elvis collects in person
Jan/Feb	A season of 57 concerts at the International Hotel, Las Vegas
27 Feb	Elvis flies to Memphis for seven days, then drives on to Nashville for a recording session
4 May	*Look* magazine features Elvis on its cover, with the first of a two-part account extracted from *Elvis: A Biography* by Jerry Hopkins
21 May	'Suspicious Minds' is named the Most Outstanding Single to be recorded in Memphis
1 Jun	The birthplace of Elvis in Tupelo is opened to the public
20 Jul	Elvis plays the first of 28 concerts at the Sahara Tahoe Hotel in Stateline, Nevada followed by another season of 57 shows at the Hilton Hotel in Las Vegas
Aug	Elvis and Priscilla move into a new house in Monovale, and Hillcrest is put up for sale
1 Sept	Elvis buys his first Stutz Blackhawk coupe – he eventually owns three
8 Sept	The Bing Crosby Award is given to Elvis by the National Academy of Recording Arts and Sciences
24 Oct	A 12-hour radio show, *The Elvis Presley Story*, is produced by Jerry Hopkins and Ron Jacobs

Nov	Elvis performs concerts in Minneapolis, Cleveland, Louisville, Philadelphia, Baltimore, Boston, Cincinnati, Houston, Dallas, Tuscaloosa, Kansas City and Salt Lake City
Nov	After Elvis passes a lie-detector test and a blood test, which prove he is not the father of Patricia Parker's son, she drops her paternity suit
30 Dec	Elvis tells his companions that Priscilla has left him
31 Dec	The *Elvis, 1971 Presley Album* is issued by *Screen Star*, with Elvis featured on every page

1972

26 Jan	The first of a new season of 57 concerts at the Las Vegas Hilton
Feb	Priscilla tells Elvis that she has been having an affair with Mike Stone
Apr	A series of concerts are played at Buffalo in New York, Detroit, Dayton, Knoxville, Hampton Roads in Virginia, Richmond, Roanoke, Indianapolis, Charlotte, Greensboro, Macon, Jacksonville, Little Rock, San Antonio and Albuquerque; many of them are filmed for the documentary *Elvis on Tour*
6 Jun	Elvis plays the opening concert of four at Madison Square Garden in New York followed by concerts in Fort Wayne and Evansville in Indiana, Milwaukee, Chicago, Fort Worth, Wichita and Tulsa
6 Jul	Elvis meets Linda Thompson, a former beauty queen
26 Jul	Elvis and Priscilla are legally separated
4 Aug	The opening concert of 63 at the Las Vegas Hilton
18 Aug	Elvis files for divorce from Priscilla
4 Sept	Elvis appears in the last in the series of Las Vegas concerts and, at a press conference, the Colonel confirms details of an NBC television special to be broadcast the following January
Sept	Linda Thompson moves into Graceland
20 Oct	Television premiere of *Change of Habit* on NBC's *Friday Night at the Movies*
1 Nov	Release of *Elvis on Tour*, which grosses nearly half a million dollars in one week
Nov	A series of concerts are played in Lubbock, Tucson, El Paso, Oakland, San Bernadino, Long Beach and Honolulu

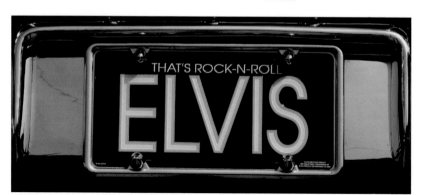

Dec A Grammy for Best Inspirational Performance is awarded for the LP 'He Touched Me'; *Elvis on Tour* is voted Best Documentary of 1972 by the Hollywood Foreign Press Association and nominated for a Golden Globe Award

1973

9 Jan Elvis arrives in Honolulu to begin rehearsals for *Elvis: Aloha From Hawaii*

14 Jan *Elvis: Aloha From Hawaii* is broadcast to 40 countries worldwide

15 Jan A second broadcast of *Elvis: Aloha From Hawaii* is seen in 28 European countries

18 Jan Elvis and his entourage fly to Las Vegas and rehearsals begin for the opening of a season in Las Vegas

26 Jan Elvis performs the opening concert of 54 at the Las Vegas Hilton

Jan Elvis gives Muhammad Ali a flamboyant, jewel-encrusted robe with 'People's Champion' inscribed across the back; Ali wears it before his 14 February fight against Joe Bugner in Las Vegas

Feb Due to the cocktail of drugs he is now taking, Elvis misses several concerts in Las Vegas and is treated by a succession of doctors

18 Feb At Elvis's midnight show, four men rush onto the stage, apparently to attack Elvis, who knocks one back into the audience; the others are removed by guards, but they turn out to be over-excited fans

23 Feb Elvis finishes the final concert in Las Vegas, but stays on to see Ann-Margret opening and several other shows

9 Mar Returning to Graceland, Elvis recuperates with Linda Thompson and the Memphis Mafia

2 Apr Elvis persuades Ed Parker to award him a sixth-degree black belt in *kenpo* karate

4 Apr *Elvis: Aloha From Hawaii* is expanded and broadcast as a TV special across the US on NBC TV

Apr Elvis persuades Kang Rhee to award him a seventh-degree black belt in *Pasaryu* karate

Apr Concerts are played in Phoenix, Anaheim, Fresno, San Diego, Portland, Spokane, Seattle and Denver

4 May Elvis is due to play 25 concerts at the Sahara Tahoe Hotel in Stateline, Nevada, but several concerts are cancelled due to illness, as years of prescription drug abuse begin to take their toll

13 May After a special Mother's Day concert, Elvis donates money to the Barton Memorial Hospital in memory of his mother

18 May Ill and exhausted, Elvis returns to Memphis

May A private investigator, John O'Grady, is hired to investigate where Elvis is getting his prescription drugs

Jun Concerts are played in Mobile, Atlanta, Uniondale, Nassau, Pittsburgh, Cincinnati, St Louis, Nashville and Oklahoma City. After returning to Memphis in July, Elvis begins a series of recording sessions

6 Aug The first concert in a planned series of 59 at the Las Vegas Hilton, although Elvis misses two due to illness

Aug After a major argument the partnership of Colonel Parker and Elvis breaks up, but is soon reinstated

9 Oct The divorce of Elvis and Priscilla is finalized in Santa Monica

Oct Elvis is hospitalized after an extreme drug reaction and is put through a drug withdrawal programme

Nov   *Movie World* features Elvis and Priscilla on its cover and reports that Elvis has collapsed after the divorce

10/16 Dec   Elvis records several songs in a session at Stax Studios in Memphis, but using a mobile recording unit provided by RCA

1974

Jan   Colonel Parker and Elvis form Boxcar Enterprises to handle the merchandizing of Elvis-related products not connected to movies or records; Boxcar Records is also created

26 Jan   The first concert in a series of 29 at the Las Vegas Hilton ending 9 February

Mar   *Silver Screen* features Elvis on its cover and an article speculates that he will marry Linda Thompson

Mar   Concerts are played in Tulsa, Houston, Monroe in Louisiana, Auburn in Alabama, Montgomery, Charlotte, Roanoke, Hampton Roads, Richmond, Greensboro, Murfreesboro in Tennessee, Knoxville and Memphis

Mar   Dr George Nichopoulos (Dr Nick) attends Elvis full time during the tour so he can monitor his drug intake

May   Concerts are played in San Bernadino, Los Angeles and Fresno followed by 22 concerts at the Sahara Tahoe Hotel in Stateline, Nevada

Jun   During a 21-day tour, concerts are played in Fort Worth, Baton Rouge, Amarillo, Des Moines, Cleveland, Providence, Philadelphia, Niagara Falls, Columbus, Louisville, Bloomington, Milwaukee, Kansas City, Omaha and Salt Lake City

19 Aug   The first concert in a planned series of 29 at the Las Vegas Hilton; Elvis is ill and has to cancel two performances

Aug   Linda Thompson is replaced by Sheila Ryan as Elvis's official girlfriend

19 Sept   Linda Thompson appears back on the scene

29 Sept   Local papers are enthusiastic after Elvis performs at the Olympian Stadium in Detroit

Oct   Concerts are played in St Paul in Minnesota, Dayton, Indianapolis, Wichita, San Antonio and Abilene followed by eight concerts at the Sahara Tahoe Hotel in Stateline, Nevada

Nov   Rolling Stone reports that Elvis is still a superstar; he wins a Grammy for Best Inspirational Performance for 'How Great Thou Art', which is featured on the LP 'Elvis Recorded Live'

Dec   Elvis recuperates from a strenuous year at Graceland and an article in *Celebrity* comments on his poor health

1975

29 Jan   Elvis is rushed to the hospital at midnight with severe stomach pains, and is admitted to get his drug use back under control

5 Feb   Elvis's father Vernon has a heart attack and is admitted to the same hospital

10/13 Mar   Elvis records at RCA's Hollywood studios

18 Mar   The first of a scheduled 29 shows at the Las Vegas Hilton

28 Mar   Barbra Streisand talks to Elvis about taking the co-starring role in the remake of *A Star is Born*, but the Colonel handles negotiations and the project founders

Apr   Elvis buys a 96-passenger Convair 880 plane, which he redecorates in blue and white, and christens the 'Lisa Marie'. It is delivered on 10 November

Apr–Jul   Concerts are played in Macon, Jacksonville, Tampa, Lakeland, Murfreesboro,

Atlanta, Monroe, Lake Charles in Louisiana, Huntsville in Alabama, Mobile, Houston, Dallas, Shreveport, Jackson, Memphis, Oklahoma City, Terre Haute in Indiana, Cleveland, Charleston, Niagara Falls, Springfield, New Haven, Uniondale, Norfolk and Greensboro

5 May Elvis plays a benefit concert at the State Fair Coliseum in Jackson, Mississippi, and raises $108,000 for hurricane survivors in McComb, Mississippi

Jul Elvis has plastic surgery to give his eyes a more youthful look

23/24 Jul During a show at Asheville, North Carolina, Elvis gives away a $6,500 ring to a fan in the audience

27 Jul After buying 14 Cadillac Eldorados, Elvis gives them all away

Aug Priscilla and Mike Stone split up; Priscilla begins her acting career; Elvis is still in poor health and is putting on weight

18 Aug Although he is due to perform a series of concerts at the Las Vegas Hilton, most of them are cancelled due to Elvis's poor health

21 Aug Elvis is admitted to the hospital for two weeks and attempts are made to solve some of his medical problems

Aug Linda Thompson leaves to pursue an acting career, and Elvis briefly sees Jo Cathy Brownlee

10 Nov The 'Lisa Marie' is finally delivered

28 Nov Elvis flies to Las Vegas to rehearse for 17 shows at the Las Vegas Hilton, and Linda Thompson returns briefly to support him

31 Dec A New Year's Eve concert in Pontiac, Michigan, breaks concert receipt records

1976

Jan Elvis buys five cars and gives them away

22 Jan A new agreement giving the Colonel 50/50 partnership on live dates comes into effect

Feb *Movie Stars* features Elvis and Linda Thompson, with an article speculating that they will marry – in fact they are already well on the way to splitting up

2–8 Feb Elvis records at Graceland, using temporary equipment installed by RCA

20 Apr Elvis invests in Presley Center Courts, Inc, which plans to run racket-ball clubs; he is a 25 per cent partner, along with his physician, Dr George Nichopoulos, Joe Esposito and real estate developer Michael McMahon; Elvis pulls out when the venture is proved to be losing money

Apr/Jun Concerts are played in Kansas City, Omaha, Denver, San Diego, Long Beach, Seattle, 15 shows at the Sahara Tahoe Hotel in Stateline, Nevada, Bloomington, Ames in Iowa, Oklahoma City, Odessa in Texas, Lubbock, Tucson, El Paso, Fort Worth, Atlanta, Omaha, Buffalo, Rhode Island, Largo in Maryland, Philadelphia, Richmond and Greensboro

13 Jul Vernon fires Red and Sonny West, along with Dave Hebler

Jul/Aug Concerts are performed at Shreveport, Baton Rouge, Fort Worth, Tulsa, Memphis, Louisville, Charleston, Syracuse, Rochester, Hartford, Springfield, New Haven, Hampton Roads, Roanoke, San Antonio, Houston, Mobile, Tuscaloosa and Macon

Sept/Oct Elvis performs concerts in Jacksonville, Florida, Alabama, Arkansas, Duluth, Minneapolis, Sioux Falls, Madison, South Bend, Kalamazoo, Champaign, Cleveland, Evansville, Fort Wayne, Dayton and Carbondale, Illinois

29 Oct	Another recording session is arranged at Graceland, but Elvis is not well enough to do much work
19 Nov	Elvis meets Ginger Alden, a former beauty queen
Nov	Billy Carter, the President's brother, comments that Elvis is guarded better than the president after he and his wife visit Graceland
Nov	Elvis performs a series of concerts in Nevada, Oregon and California, and Ginger Alden is invited to join him; Linda Thompson finally leaves for good
2 Dec	A new season of 15 concerts begins at the Las Vegas Hilton; the last is on December 12, and this time Elvis does not miss any performances
Dec	Elvis gives Ginger a Lincoln Mark V
9 Dec	Vernon is admitted to the hospital with a suspected heart attack
27 Dec	The first of five concerts is performed in Wichita, Kansas; the others are in Texas, Alabama, Georgia and Pennsylvania

1977

Jan	Priscilla and Elvis are featured on the cover of *TV Star Parade*, with an article speculating that they have secretly remarried
Jan	Elvis spends his birthday with Ginger and her sister Rosemary in Palm Springs
20 Jan	A recording session is scheduled in Nashville, but Elvis cancels due to a sore throat
26 Jan	Elvis proposes to Ginger and gives her a diamond ring
1 Feb	Elvis and Ginger celebrate Lisa Marie's ninth birthday with her in Los Angeles
Feb–Mar	A series of 17 concerts are played in Florida, Alabama, Georgia, South Carolina, Tennessee, North Carolina, Arizona, Texas, Oklahoma and Louisiana
3 Mar	Elvis takes Ginger and her family on a two-week holiday to Hawaii
Apr	A series of concerts is booked through North Carolina, Michigan, Ohio, Wisconsin, Minnesota and Illinois, but Elvis collapses during the tour, and is taken back to Memphis and admitted to the Baptist Memorial Hospital
5 Apr	Elvis leaves the hospital and spends some time recuperating at Graceland
Apr	Elvis argues with Ginger and invites Alicia Kerwin to accompany him on a trip to Las Vegas and Palm Springs
May/Jun	A series of 23 concerts is performed across 18 states with only 16 days' rest during the punishing schedule; Ginger accompanies Elvis for most of the time
May	Newspapers report that the Colonel is planning to sell Elvis's contract to pay off his gambling debts
1 Jun	The Colonel announces details of an upcoming CBS concert special, to be filmed on the next tour
18 Jun	*Photoplay* awards Elvis Gold Medal Awards for Favourite Variety Star and Favourite Rock Music Star
27 Jun	Elvis returns to Graceland to recuperate
Jul	Release of 'Way Down'/'Pledging My Love', which goes into the *Billboard* country chart for 17 weeks, reaching No. 1 in August; it also spends 21 weeks in the Top 100 chart, reaching No. 18, and reaches No. 14 on the easy listening chart; in the UK it becomes Elvis's 17th No. 1 record
Jul	The book, *Elvis: What Happened?*, is published, written by Steve Dunleavy and based on material from the three ex-members of the Memphis Mafia: Red West, Sonny West and Dave Hebler

Jul/Aug   Lisa Marie arrives at Graceland for a two-week visit; Elvis rents the Libertyland amusement park for several hours after closing time as a present for Lisa Marie and her friends

16 Aug   Elvis is found dead in his bathroom at Graceland by Ginger Alden; the cause of death is announced as a heart attack, but the later autopsy rules that he died from a drug overdose

17 Aug   With his body lying in state at Graceland, thousands of fans congregate outside, waiting to file past the coffin and get one last glimpse of Elvis

18 Aug   Elvis's funeral is held at Graceland, and he is laid to rest next to his mother at Forest Hill Cemetery

23 Aug   The Colonel convinces Vernon to sign a contract giving all rights to the marketing of Elvis-related products to Boxcar Enterprises; 50 per cent of income to be distributed equally between the Colonel and the Elvis Presley estate, with the remaining 50 per cent for expenses and salaries; anything left after expenses to be divided 56 per cent to the Colonel and the rest between the estate and Tom Diskin

21 Aug   RCA reports that it has sold over eight million Elvis records in the six days since his death

29 Aug   Three men attempt to steal Elvis's body; charges are later dropped when the court believes they were trying to prove the coffin was empty and that Elvis was still alive

7 Sept   A shorter version of the documentary E*lvis on Tour* is shown on NBC TV to top ratings

12 Sept   'Way Down' is certified gold by the RIAA

3 Oct   CBS TV shows *Elvis in Concert*, a one-hour special that was filmed during his last tour

27 Oct   The bodies of Elvis and his mother are removed from Forest Hill Cemetery and re-interred at Graceland in the Meditation Garden

Nov   Elvis's physician, Doctor Nichopoulos suspended while the court investigates his prescription of drugs to Elvis

Nov   A Broadway show, *Elvis Lives*, wins the *New York Evening Standard* award for Best Musical of the Year

20 Nov   A three-hour television special, *Memories of Elvis*, is broadcast on NBC TV

1978

Jan   Elvis has left his entire estate to Lisa Marie, but Priscilla and the other trustees are horrified to discover there is no money left

1 Feb   *Playboy* inducts Elvis into its Music Hall of Fame

16/18 Aug   On the first anniversary of Elvis's death, thousands of fans gather outside Graceland

1/10 Sept   An Elvis Presley Convention is held at the Las Vegas Hilton – it becomes an annual event

8 Sept   A bronze statue of Elvis is unveiled in the lobby of the Las Vegas Hilton

1979

Jan   Investigations into Elvis's finances reveal he was not a member of Broadcast Music Inc, and so had probably lost millions of dollars in royalty payments

8 Jan   The anniversary of Elvis's birth is celebrated in Memphis and Tupelo, and becomes an annual event

11 Feb   ABC TV broadcasts *Elvis*, the story of his life with Kurt Russell playing Elvis and Shelley Winters as Gladys

Apr   A newsletter about Elvis, called *Reflections*, is started by two ex-members of the Memphis Mafia

May	Two tons of grey marble from Elvis's first tomb at the Forest Hill Cemetery are bought by Bill Carwile; he cuts it up into 44,000 small pieces, which he sells for $80 each
26 Jun	Vernon dies of heart failure, and is later buried next to Elvis and Gladys
17 Aug	An Elvis Presley Chapel is dedicated in Elvis Presley Park in Tupelo

1980

8 Feb	NBC TV broadcasts *Elvis Remembered: Nashville to Hollywood*, which is a shortened version of *Nashville Remembers Elvis On His Birthday*
8 May	Minnie Mae Presley, Elvis's grandmother, dies in Memphis
24 Jun	Singer Margot Heine Kuzma alleges in the German Globe that her son Leroy is the son of Elvis

1981

	The IRS claims that Elvis's estate owes $14.6 million in inheritance taxes, plus a further $2.3 million in tax interest; to raise funds and protect her daughter's inheritance, Priscilla plans to open Graceland to the public
3 Apr	Premiere in Memphis of a documentary, *This is Elvis*, made by Warner Brothers
Jul	The courts decide that Boxcar Enterprises has no right to distribute Elvis-related merchandise
Jul/Aug	At the Las Vegas Hilton, *Elvis, An American Musical* is performed

1982

7 Jun	The downstairs rooms at Graceland are opened to the public
Oct	Release of 'The Elvis Medley', which goes on to stay in the *Billboard* Top LPs chart for nine weeks

1983

8 Jan	An Elvis Presley Museum is opened in London

1984

Aug	*Life* runs an article pointing out that the Elvis Presley industry is earning ten times as much as he did when he was alive
Aug/Nov	The interior of Graceland is filmed for a video, *Elvis Presley's Graceland*; Elvis is posthumously awarded the WC Handy Award from the Blues Foundation for 'keeping the blues alive'; Elvis is also posthumously awarded the first Golden Hat Award from the Academy of Country Music for his influence on country music

1985

5 Jan	A TV special, *Elvis: One Night With You* – a complete record of one of the performances taped for the NBC TV Elvis comeback special – is shown on Home Box Office cable TV and repeated throughout the month
Aug	A syndicated TV special, *Elvis: The Echo Will Never Die*, features people who knew or worked with Elvis

1986

Feb	Elvis is, posthumously, one of the first to be inducted into the Rock and Roll Hall of Fame in Cleveland, Ohio

1987

Aug	On a phone-in run by *USA Today*, fans vote 'Suspicious Minds' their No. 1 favourite Elvis song, with 'Love Me Tender' No. 2
	Elvis is posthumously granted an Award of Merit at the American Music Awards

1988

The 1956 recording of 'Hound Dog' is inducted into the NARAS Hall of Fame

7/8 Feb   A mini-series, *Elvis and Me*, based on Priscilla's book about her life with Elvis, is broadcast on ABC TV and becomes the highest-rated TV movie of 1987/88

Oct   Lisa Marie marries musician Danny Keough

1989

NBC TV broadcasts *Elvis: Comeback 68* – a repeat of the programme broadcast on 3 December 1968, which *TV Guide* describes as the best rock performance ever on television

29 May   Lisa Marie and her husband have a daughter, Danielle Riley

1990

May   The first Elvis Awards ceremony is held in New York, and Eric Clapton is named Best Rock Guitarist

1992

A two-volume video collection is re-edited and broadcast as *Elvis, The Great Performances (Televised Version)*, with Priscilla hosting it from Graceland

A video, *Elvis, The Lost Performances*, is released, with unseen footage from the films of his concerts

22 Jan   A two-hour TV special, *The Elvis Conspiracy – The Elvis Files*, is broadcast; it alleges that Elvis went undercover for the FBI and is still alive

6 Apr   A postcard ballot is held to choose which image of Elvis is to be used on a US postage stamp; an image of a young Elvis is chosen. *US News &*

World Report says that revenue from sales of the Elvis stamp is expected to reach $20 million. The stamp is released in January 1993 and becomes the best-selling stamp in US postal history

21 Oct   Lisa Marie and her husband have a second child, a boy named Benjamin Storm

1993

A video documentary, *Elvis in Hollywood*, is released, including footage from the first four movies, out-takes, and interviews with those involved at the time

A TV special, *America Comes to Graceland*, about Elvis's life and legacy, is broadcast in the US

1 Feb   Lisa Marie turns 25 and is entitled to take charge of her inheritance, but decides to found the Elvis Presley Trust to run the estate, with Priscilla and the National Bank of Commerce as co-trustees

1 Mar   *People* magazine estimates that Elvis's estate is now worth nearly $100 million

1994

Lisa Marie divorces Danny Keough

26 May   Michael Jackson and Lisa Marie are married in the Dominican Republic

1995

The 1956 recording of 'Heartbreak Hotel' is inducted into the NARAS Hall of Fame

1996

Lisa Marie divorces Michael Jackson

A virtual tour of Graceland is released on CD

1997

At the Mid-South Coliseum in Memphis, *Elvis in Concert, 97* features Elvis on video accompanied live on stage by over 30 of his former band members and the Memphis Symphony Orchestra; a digitally remastered video is also shown, with Lisa Marie singing 'Don't Cry, Daddy' with Elvis

An official video tour, *Elvis Presley's Graceland*, is released

1998

The 1954 recording of 'That's All Right, Mama' is inducted into the NARAS Hall of Fame

Lisa Marie becomes owner and Chairman of the Board of Elvis Presley Enterprises, Inc, while Priscilla becomes Chairman of the Advisory Board

Elvis is posthumously inducted into the Country Music Hall of Fame

1999

The 1969 recording of 'Suspicious Minds' is inducted into the NARAS Hall of Fame

Nov/Jan A two-part documentary, *He Touched Me: The Gospel Music of Elvis Presley*, is aired on TNN and the entire programme is also released as two videos

2001

21 Sept 'America The Beautiful', a special CD single featuring Elvis singing three songs, enters the *Billboard* Hot 100 singles sales chart at No. 8; it peaks at No. 6 for two weeks in November

Dec Graceland is voted fourth Most Visited Historic House Museum in the United States, on the list compiled by the Almanac of Architecture and Design; Elvis is posthumously inducted into the Gospel Music Hall of Fame

2002

9 Jan It is announced that the Vaughan-Bassett Furniture Company has gone into partnership with Elvis Presley Enterprises, Inc to manufacture an exclusive range of wood furniture to be known as the Elvis Presley Collection.

ACKNOWLEDGMENTS

All photographs in this book are reproduced by kind permission of
Aquarius Collection Limited and Corbis.

1	Bettman, Corbis
2	Bettman, Corbis
3	Bettman, Corbis
4	Aquarius
5	Corbis
6	Corbis
8	Aquarius
9	Bettman, Corbis

CHAPTER 1

10–11	Bettman, Corbis
12	Bettman, Corbis
16	Corbis
20	Corbis
21	Corbis
22	Corbis
23 t	Bettman, Corbis
23 b	Bettman, Corbis
24	Aquarius
25	Aquarius
26–27	Bettman, Corbis
28	Aquarius
29	Bettman, Corbis
30	Bettman, Corbis
31	Bettman, Corbis
32–33	Bettman, Corbis
34	Bettman, Corbis
35	Bettman, Corbis
36 t	Bettman, Corbis
36 b	Bettman, Corbis
37	Bettman, Corbis
38	Bettman, Corbis
39 t	Corbis
39 b	Bettman, Corbis
40 R	Corbis
41	Bettman, Corbis
42	Corbis
43	Corbis
44	Twentieth Century Fox/ Aquarius
45	Twentieth Century Fox/ Aquarius
46	Twentieth Century Fox/ Aquarius
47 t	Bettman, Corbis
47 b	Corbis
48	Corbis
49	Corbis
50	Bettman, Corbis
51	Bettman, Corbis
52	Corbis
53	Corbis
54	Corbis
55	Bettman, Corbis
56	Bettman, Corbis
57	Bettman, Corbis
58	Bettman, Corbis
59	Bettman, Corbis
60	Bettman, Corbis
61	Bettman, Corbis
62	Bettman, Corbis
63	Twentieth Century Fox/ Aquarius
64	Corbis
65	Corbis
66	Corbis

67 t	Corbis
67 b	Corbis

CHAPTER 2

68–69	Bettman, Corbis
70	Bettman, Corbis
73	Bettman, Corbis
76 t	Corbis
76 b	Bettman, Corbis
77	Bettman, Corbis
78	Bettman, Corbis
79	Aquarius
80	Bettman, Corbis
81	MGM/Aquarius
82	Bettman, Corbis
83	MGM/Aquarius
84	Bettman, Corbis
85 t	Underwood and Underwood, Corbis
85 b	Bettman, Corbis
86	Bettman, Corbis
87	Bettman, Corbis
88	Bettman, Corbis
89 t	MGM/Aquarius
89 b	Bettman, Corbis
90	Bettman, Corbis
91	Corbis
92	Bettman, Corbis
93	Corbis
94	Corbis
95	Corbis
96–97	MGM/Aquarius
98 t	Seattle Post-Intelligencer Collection; Museum of History and Industry, Corbis
98 b	MGM/Aquarius
99	Bettman, Corbis

CHAPTER 3

100–101	Bettman, Corbis
102	Bettman, Corbis
108	Paramount/Aquarius
109	Bettman, Corbis
110	Bettman, Corbis
111	Bettman, Corbis
112	Bettman, Corbis
113	Bettman, Corbis
114	Bettman, Corbis
115	Bettman, Corbis
116	Bettman, Corbis
117 L	Corbis
117 R	Bettman, Corbis
118	Bettman, Corbis
119 t	Bettman, Corbis
119 b	Corbis
120–121	Bettman, Corbis
122 t	Bettman, Corbis
122 b	Bettman, Corbis
123	Bettman, Corbis
124	Bettman, Corbis
125	Bettman, Corbis
126	Bettman, Corbis
127	Aquarius

128	Bettman, Corbis
129	Bettman, Corbis
130	Corbis
131	Bettman, Corbis
132	Bettman, Corbis
133	Bettman, Corbis
134	Corbis
135	Bettman, Corbis
136	Corbis
137	Bettman, Corbis
138	Bettman, Corbis
139	Bettman, Corbis
140	Bettman, Corbis
141	Corbis
142	Bettman, Corbis
143	Bettman, Corbis
144 t	Bettman, Corbis
144 b	Corbis
145	Bettman, Corbis
146	Bettman, Corbis
147 t	Bettman, Corbis
147 b	Bettman, Corbis
148	Aquarius
149	Bettman, Corbis
150	Aquarius
151 t	Bettman, Corbis
151 b	Bettman, Corbis
152	Bettman, Corbis
153	Bettman, Corbis
154	Bettman, Corbis
155	Corbis
156 t	Bettman, Corbis
156 b	Bettman, Corbis
157	Bettman, Corbis
158	Corbis
159	Bettman, Corbis
160	Paramount/Aquarius
161	Bettman, Corbis
162–163	Paramount/Aquarius
164	Paramount/Aquarius
165	Paramount/Aquarius
166	Paramount/Aquarius
167	Bettman, Corbis
168	Bettman, Corbis
169	Paramount/Aquarius
170	Twentieth Century Fox/ Aquarius
171	Twentieth Century Fox/ Aquarius
172	Twentieth Century Fox/ Aquarius
173	Twentieth Century Fox/ Aquarius
174 t	Twentieth Century Fox/ Aquarius
174 b	Twentieth Century Fox/ Aquarius
175	Bettman, Corbis
176	Aquarius
177 t	Bettman, Corbis
177 b	Bettman, Corbis

CHAPTER 4

178–179	Bettman, Corbis
180	Twentieth Century Fox/ Aquarius
182	Twentieth Century Fox/ Aquarius
186	Twentieth Century Fox/ Aquarius
188	Bettman, Corbis

189	Corbis
190	Bettman, Corbis
191 t	Bettman, Corbis
191 b	Hal B. Wallis, Paramount/Aquarius
192	Bettman, Corbis
193	Bettman, Corbis
194	Paramount/Aquarius
195 t	Bettman, Corbis
195 b	Bettman, Corbis
196	United Artists/Aquarius
197 t	Bettman, Corbis
197 b	Bettman, Corbis
198	Bettman, Corbis
199	Paramount/Aquarius
200	Corbis
201	Corbis
202	Seattle Post-Intelligencer Collection; Museum of History and Industry; Corbis
203	Seattle Post-Intelligencer Collection; Museum of History and Industry, Corbis
204	MGM/Aquarius
205	Paramount/Aquarius
206–207	Bettman, Corbis
208	Bettman, Corbis
209 t	Bettman, Corbis
209 b	MGM/Aquarius
210	MGM/Aquarius
211	Aquarius
212	Aquarius
213	Bettman, Corbis
214–215	Bettman, Corbis
216	Bettman, Corbis
217	Bettman, Corbis
218	Paramount/Aquarius
219 t	Paramount/Aquarius
219 b	Allied Artists/Aquarius
220	Allied Artists/Aquarius
221	Allied Artists/Aquarius
222	Allied Artists/Aquarius
223 t	Allied Artists/Aquarius
223 b	Allied Artists/Aquarius
224 t	Allied Artists/Aquarius
224 b	Allied Artists/Aquarius
225	Allied Artists/Aquarius
226	Allied Artists/Aquarius
227	Allied Artists/Aquarius
228	MGM/Aquarius
229	United Artists/Aquarius
230	Aquarius
231	Bettman, Corbis
232 t	MGM/Aquarius
232 b	Bettman, Corbis
233	Bettman, Corbis
234	MGM/Aquarius
235	MGM/Aquarius
236	MGM/Aquarius
237	United Artists/Aquarius
238–239	Bettman, Corbis
240	Bettman, Corbis
241	Bettman, Corbis
242	Bettman, Corbis
243	Bettman, Corbis
244 t	Aquarius
244 b	Bettman, Corbis
245	Bettman, Corbis
246	MGM/Aquarius
247 t	MGM/Aquarius
247 b	MGM/Aquarius
248	MGM/Aquarius
249	MGM/Aquarius
250	MGM/Aquarius
251 t	MGM/Aquarius
251 b	Bettman, Corbis
252	Bettman, Corbis
253	Bettman, Corbis
254 t	MGM/Aquarius
254 b	MGM/Aquarius
255	MGM/Aquarius
256	Bettman, Corbis
257	Sygma
258	Sygma
259 t	Sygma
259 b	Sygma
260 t	MGM/Aquarius
260 b	MGM/Aquarius
261	MGM/Aquarius
262	MGM/Aquarius
263 t	MGM/Aquarius
263 b	MGM/Aquarius
264 t	MGM/Aquarius
264 b	Bettman, Corbis
265	MGM/Aquarius
266	Aquarius
267 t	National General, Aquarius
267 b	National General, Aquarius
268	National General, Aquarius
269 t	MGM/Aquarius
269 b	MGM/Aquarius
270	Aquarius
271	Aquarius
272	Bettman, Corbis
273	Bettman, Corbis
274	Bettman, Corbis
275	Universal/Aquarius
276	Bettman, Corbis
277	Frank Carroll, Sygma
278	Frank Carroll, Sygma
279 t	Frank Carroll, Sygma
279 b	Frank Carroll, Sygma
280	Frank Carroll, Sygma
281	Frank Carroll, Sygma

CHAPTER 5

282–283	Bettman, Corbis
284	Spatz, Sygma
286	Bettman, Corbis
290	Sam Emerson, Sygma
291	MGM/Aquarius
292–293	Bettman, Corbis
294	Frank Carroll, Sygma
295	Frank Carroll, Sygma
296	Frank Carroll, Sygma
297 t	Frank Carroll, Sygma
297 b	Frank Carroll, Sygma
298	Frank Carroll, Sygma
299	Frank Carroll, Sygma
300 t	Corbis
300 b	Frank Carroll, Sygma
301	Frank Carroll, Sygma
302	Frank Carroll, Sygma
303	Frank Carroll, Sygma
304 t	Frank Carroll, Sygma
304 b	Frank Carroll, Sygma
305	Frank Carroll, Sygma
306–307	Korody, Sygma
308	Bettman, Corbis
309	Bettman, Corbis
310	Bettman, Corbis
311	Jeff Albertson, Corbis
312	Bettman, Corbis
313 t	Jeff Albertson, Corbis
313 b	Bettman, Corbis
314 t	Bettman, Corbis
314 b	Bettman, Corbis
315	Bettman, Corbis
316	Bettman, Corbis
317	Aquarius
318	Bettman, Corbis
319	Bettman, Corbis
320	Bettman, Corbis
321b	Bettman, Corbis
322	Bettman, Corbis
323	Lynn Goldsmith, Corbis
324	Bettman, Corbis
325	Bettman, Corbis
326	Aquarius
327 t	Bettman, Corbis
327 b	Bettman, Corbis

CHAPTER 6

328–329	Bettman, Corbis
330	Bettman, Corbis
334 t	Bettman, Corbis
334 b	Bettman, Corbis
335	Bettman, Corbis
336 t	Bettman, Corbis
336 b	Roger Garwood and Trish Ainslie, Corbis
337	Henry Diltz, Corbis
338	Bettman, Corbis
339	Franz-Marc Frei, Corbis
340	Roger Garwood and Trish Ainslie, Corbis
341 t	Kevin Fleming, Corbis
341 b	Kevin Fleming, Corbis
342–343	Arthur Grace, Sygma
343 (inset)	Henry Diltz, Corbis
344 t	Dave Bartruff, Corbis
344 b	Philip Gould, Corbis
345	Alain Nogues, Sygma
346 t	Jan Butchofsky-Houser, Corbis
346 b	Raymond Gehman, Corbis
347	Kevin Fleming, Corbis

BIBLIOGRAPHY AND FACTS

348	Corbis
349	Aquarius
350–351	Paramount/Aquarius
352	Paramount/Aquarius
353 t	Aquarius
353 b	Corbis

CHRONOLOGY

354	Aquarius
359	Aquarius
367	Paramount/Aquarius
372	Corbis
381	Corbis

Every effort has been made to ensure that the copyright details shown are correct, but if there are any inaccuracies, please contact the publisher.